TALKING BALLS

TALKING BALLS

A GUIDE TO THE LANGUAGE OF SPORT

ANDREW DELAHUNTY

FOREWORD BY SKY SPORTS' JEFF STELLING

WEIDENFELD & NICOLSON

First published in Great Britain in 2006
by Weidenfeld & Nicolson

1 3 5 6 7 9 10 8 6 4 2

A CIP catalogue record for this book is available
from the British Library.

ISBN-13: 978 0 304 36818 1
ISBN-10: 0 304 36818 0

Printed and bound in Great Britain by Clays Ltd, St Ives plc

Weidenfeld & Nicolson
The Orion Publishing Group Ltd
Orion House
5 Upper St Martin's Lane
London WC2H 9EA
www.orionbooks.co.uk

The Orion Publishing Group's policy is to use papers that are natural, renewable and
recyclable products and made from wood grown in sustainable forests. The logging
and manufacturing processes are expected to conform to the environmental
regulations of the country of origin.

Foreword

What makes the language of sport so special?

On first consideration, sporting terminology can seem to be far removed from its supposed meaning – 'handbags' for a petty squabble or scuffle, to 'tickle' a ball in cricket, golf's 'albatross' or baseball's 'round the horn' – but when considered such terms allow us to describe a complex play or act in the most concise language.

In *Talking Balls*, Andrew Delahunty has done just that in what is a fascinating and joyous guide to the language of sport. Not only does he reveal sporting terms and meanings that were new to me but also the enthralling stories behind them.

The study of any one language of sport is absorbing but only when a collection of sports are viewed together in this form, as they are here, can the themes and links across all sports be truly enjoyed and appreciated.

Jeff Stelling
SEPTEMBER 2006

Introduction

'There's pace on the bench', I heard a football commentator observe the other day, and was struck by this elegantly, almost poetically, succinct way of saying that the team's substitutes included a number of players noted for their speed. I often find myself admiring the economy and vividness of the language used to talk about sport. And, watching a match on TV with friends, I sometimes find that, while everyone else is quite properly engrossed in the unfolding sporting drama, I have become distracted pondering the sheer oddness of talking about a striker receiving a *square ball* or a batsman playing a shot with *soft hands* or, afterwards, hearing a rugby player bemoaning a *bad day at the office*. This is, alas, what happens when you follow sport as a lexicographer, but I don't think you have to write dictionaries for a living to relish encountering all those curious words and phrases that are such an integral part of the pleasure of watching sport. The pleasure, that is, of *nurdle* and *oche* and *yips*.

Talking Balls sets out to celebrate the rich, quirky, and colourful language of sport and explain the meaning and origin of hundreds of terms and phrases currently used in sportspeak. What is a batsman up to when he *farms the strike*, plays an *agricultural shot*, or does some *gardening*? What is the *B of the Bang*? And *Row Z*? Where do the words *deuce*, *dormie*, and *doosra* come from? What is the difference between the *tail wagging* in cricket and *wagging the tail* in horse racing? What is the literal meaning of all those exotic foreign words we use in sport, such as *galactico*, *peloton*, and *repêchage*? I have concentrated on terms and expressions that are gloriously odd-sounding in their own right or that have intriguing origins or striking patterns of use.

The book includes many everyday expressions that originated from some sporting context, such as *ball is in your court, ballpark figure, behind the eight ball, body blow, down to the wire*, etc. A selection of familiar allusions (the *Ball of the Century, the Russian linesman*) and celebrated quotations ('*Your boys took one hell of a beating*', '*Say it ain't so, Joe*') are also covered. In addition, dotted around the text are a number of thematic panels on particular aspects of sports language, such as the language of relegation, the post-match interview, the use of metaphors from warfare in sport.

The germ of this book was a number of enjoyable discussions with fellow-lexicographer Ramesh Krishnamurthy on *six-pointer* and other footballing expressions, and Ramesh later also offered useful comments on some of the draft entries. My thanks go too to Graham Howard for his excellent suggestions for horse-racing entries to include and to Stephen Mackey for his contribution to one of the football entries. I have benefited from the encouragement of two editors at Weidenfeld & Nicolson, Richard Milbank, who did much to shape the content and style of this book in the early stages and whose enthusiastic comments on the text were invaluable, and Matt Lowing who took over the reins at a later stage and ably guided the book to publication.

Andrew Delahunty
SEPTEMBER 2006

a

ace

In tennis, an **ace** is a winning serve that the opposing player fails to reach. Since a point is won with a single stroke, this meaning can be seen as an extension of the idea of a playing card with a single symbol on it. **Ace** can also be used as a verb, as in 'he aced me with his first serve of the match'. A player who hits more aces than his or her opponent **out-aces** them: 'Federer out-aced Roddick 11–7.' For golfers, an **ace** is a hole-in-one, that is, when a tee shot lands in the hole. Here, too, the word can also be used as a verb: 'She aced the 130-yard 12th hole.'

address

In golf jargon, to **address** the ball is to adopt a particular stance in preparation for striking the ball with a golf club. According to the old joke, when told by his instructor to address the ball, the novice golfer responds by saying, 'Hello, ball', or, in another version, takes out a pen and writes 'To green' on the ball.

advantage

Advantage has a specific meaning in tennis, indicating that a player has scored the next point after deuce (a score of 40–40). The idea is that the same player needs only to score one more point to win the game. The **advantage court** (informally known as the **ad court**) is the left side of the court for each player.

● agricultural shot

Not to be confused with **farming the strike**, an **agricultural shot** in cricket is a hefty and inelegant swipe with the bat, usually one that sends the ball airborne: 'The tail-ender attempted an agricultural shot and was caught on the boundary.' The image is of someone swinging a scythe or some other farming tool.
See also COW CORNER, COW SHOT.

● air ball

In basketball, an **air ball** is an embarrassing attempted shot that misses the basket completely, failing to hit the net, rim or backboard.

● albatross

Albatross is a British golf term for a score of three under par on a particular hole. It is an extension of the bird theme, where a 'birdie' is a score of one under par and an 'eagle' is two under par. Basically, the birds get bigger and rarer. In US English, the usual term is 'double eagle'. *See also* BIRDIE, EAGLE.

● alley-oop

In basketball, an **alley-oop** (or **alley-oop pass**) is a pass thrown high in the air to a point just over the basket so that a teammate who is running towards the basket can jump up to catch the ball in mid-air, immediately scoring a basket before he lands. This colourful expression takes its name from a 1930s comic strip character called Alley Oop (whose name punned on the French cry *allez-oop*, associated with circus acrobats and trapeze artists). He was a caveman who, Tarzan-like, swung from tree to tree on vines.

● also-ran

The term **also-ran**, meaning a person of no importance or distinction, a loser, comes from racing. It properly denotes a horse, dog, etc. that finishes outside the first three places in a race.

● anchor

A number of sports make use of nautical terminology, particularly baseball. In athletics, the member of a relay team who runs the last leg is known as the **anchor**. *See also* AROUND THE HORN, ON DECK, WHEELHOUSE.

● ankle breaker

Ankle breaker is a wincingly descriptive piece of basketball slang for a move involving such a quick change of direction that it completely wrong-foots a defender and forces him to shift his body weight with such speed that you could imagine he'd be in serious danger of breaking his ankle.

● ankle tap

In rugby, an **ankle tap** (also called a **tap tackle**) is a tackle made by diving and tripping up a player by grabbing his ankle with your hands. Often a last-ditch attempt to prevent a try being scored, the term tends to be preceded by an adjective such as 'despairing', 'desperate' or 'crucial'.

● Annie's room

In darts, the term **Annie's room** is colloquially used to say that a player needs double 1. The phrase 'up in Annie's room' dates back to the First World War when it was used as a vague answer to a question regarding a missing person's whereabouts. The idea is that the person isn't where he is supposed to be, just like a darts player whose failure to throw earlier doubles has left him where he shouldn't be either, trying to throw double 1.

● answers

Sportsmen often talk about overcoming resistance or responding to setbacks in terms of being asked questions and coming up with **answers**:

England's Andy Robinson, in particular, was encouraged that his side had found answers to some tricky early questions. Guardian, 13/2/06

It's no wonder that international contests in cricket and rugby are known as Tests. In US basketball, the player Allen Iverson is nicknamed '**The Answer**' because his scoring ability is thought to be able to provide the answer to problems posed by the opposing team.

● areas

In the context of cricket, the **areas** (specifically 'good areas' or 'the right areas') are the places where the bowler pitches the ball, especially when the pressure of consistent accuracy makes it difficult for the batsman to score runs:

It's not just about bowling fast, you still have to put the ball in good areas. Chris Silverwood, 12/11/02

We haven't bowled enough in the right areas. Nasser Hussain, 18/12/02

● around the horn

To throw (or 'toss' or 'whip' or 'work') the ball **around the horn** in baseball is to execute a manoeuvre in which the ball is thrown first from the fielder at third base to second base and then from second to first, in so doing putting out the runners (in what is called a double play) at both second and first base. The term comes from sailing: before the Panama Canal was opened in 1914, the quickest route from the north Atlantic to the Pacific was sailing around Cape Horn, the southern extremity of South America. The region is notorious for its gales and heavy seas and 'rounding the Horn' was a hazardous undertaking in a sailing ship.

After Wilkerson struck out swinging for the first out of the fourth,
catcher Closser tried to whip the ball around the horn, but his toss
sailed into the outfield. usatoday.com, 20/7/05

Third baseman Ramon Martinez started a snappy around-the-horn
double play when he fielded Joe Crede's second-inning smash.
chicagotribune.com, 4/7/04

● arrows

Darts are informally known as **arrows** and, in much the same
way as **hoops** can mean basketball, the word can also mean the
game of darts.

● assist

When a player passes or throws the ball or puck to set up a
teammate to score a goal or (in baseball) put out an opposing
batter, this contribution is known as an **assist**, especially when it
is officially recorded. The term was originally used in such North
American sports as ice hockey, basketball and baseball, but is now
common in football too, particularly since the advent of fantasy
football competitions.

● attack

Many sports, especially team games, are based on the idea of
attacking and defending. In cycling, though, to **attack** has a
more specific meaning. It's what a rider does when he suddenly
accelerates in a bid to pull away from another rider or a pack of
riders.

● attack the net

Tennis umpires can deduct points from players or impose fines for
'racket abuse' and other forms of unsportsmanlike conduct.
Attacking the net sounds as though it might fall into the same
category, but the expression describes not an act of on-court

violence but a tactic during play, by which a player quickly advances to the front of the court towards the net so that he or she is in a position to hit volleys:

Federer lost his opening service game, but afterwards attacked the net at key moments to break the Spaniard's serve. sportsillustrated.cnn.com, 12/6/03

● autobus

They are known as the **autobus** (in French) or the **gruppetto** (in Italian) or the **laughing group**. Who are they? They are a group of cyclists, usually the sprinters as opposed to the climbing specialists, who all stick together during the gruelling mountain stages of races such as the Tour de France in order to help one another finish within the time limit and so avoid being disqualified.

● away to our left/right

Football commentators, especially on radio, are fond of the phrase **away to our left/right** when describing the scene. Presumably intended to convey a sense of the vastness of the stadium, it has become a familiar verbal tic.

b

back door

In golf, the **back door** (also called the **tradesman's entrance**) is the rear of the hole from the point of view of a player making a putt. So if the putt curls around the hole before it drops in from the back, it is said to 'go in by the back door'.

back nine

The **back nine** is the second half of a round of golf, consisting of the final nine holes numbered 10 to 18: 'He made three birdies on the back nine.' *See also* FRONT NINE.

back stick

In football, the **back stick** is a more informal way of referring to the far post, that is, the goalpost farthest away from where the ball is being played from, especially when a corner kick is being taken. *See also* BETWEEN THE STICKS.

back to square one

Strictly speaking, the phrase **back to square one**, meaning 'back to where you started, with no progress made', shouldn't be included here, as its origin may well not have any connection with sport at all. It is commonly believed, though, that the phrase derives from the early days of radio commentaries on football matches, when a diagram of the football pitch was printed in the *Radio Times* and divided into a grid of numbered sections so that listeners could follow the progress of the ball during the course of the match. More likely, however, is that the phrase relates to games like hopscotch or board games of the snakes-and-ladders variety.

● back yourself

It is increasingly common to hear sportspeople, especially cricketers, talk about **backing myself** or **backing ourselves**, that is, having confidence in their own ability. The expression is a variation on 'to bet' or 'to put money on' as a way of suggesting confidence in a particular outcome:

I think we'd back ourselves to bowl them out on that wicket. Jacques Kallis, 5/3/2000

I was disappointed with my form in the summer as I back myself to be a good player. Ian Bell, 13/11/2005

● bad day at the office

Increasingly a staple of the post-match interview (or, more specifically, the post-defeat interview), **a bad day at the office** is a rueful acknowledgement of a poor performance. There is something wildly incongruous about, say, a hulking, mud-spattered rugby player presenting himself as he trudges off the pitch as an ordinary nine-to-fiver, just home from his day's work attending to his in-tray.

It was a bad day at the office for me – two touches and a capsize at the bottom. I'm a little subdued. My goal was gold. Paul Ratcliffe, British Olympic canoeist, 20/9/2000

It was a bad day at the office. We had six or seven players that didn't perform. Steve McClaren, 6/3/05

● bagel

Sport is full of food-related expressions, such as **pie-throwing** (cricket), **fried egg** (golf), **meat in the sandwich** (horse racing) and **can of corn** (baseball). A contribution to this linguistic hamper from tennis is **bagel**. This is an informal term for a set that is won six games to love (that is, 6–0), the shape of the zero suggesting that of a bagel. Two such sets are a **double bagel**. To **bagel** a set is to win it without losing any games:

Hingis Double Bagels Opponent headline referring to 6–0 6–0 victory over Cho Yoon-Jeong at Pan Pacific Open, protennisfan.com, 1/2/06

The term appears to have first been used in the 1970s in connection with the US doubles partners Eddie Dibbs and Harold Solomon, dubbed the 'Bagel Twins' by TV commentator Bud Collins because they were both assumed to be Jewish and the bagel is the quintessential Jewish food. In fact, while Solomon was indeed Jewish, Dibbs was of Lebanese extraction. It was probably Dibbs, though, who first described a 6–0 set as a 'bagel job'. The alternatives **donut** and **double donut** are sometimes used in US English. *See also* BREADSTICK.

● bag o' nuts

In darts slang, **bag o' nuts** is a score of 45, apparently because in the 1930s such a score on a fairground darts stall would win the thrower a bag of nuts.

● bail out

To **bail out** in golf is to avoid trouble by playing safe, for example by choosing to aim away from a hazard such as a bunker: 'There is a bail-out area to the right of the green.'

● ball is in your court

If the **ball is in your court**, it is up to you to make the next move. The expression derives, of course, from tennis.

LO-OVE

There is a rich variety of ways of saying 'no score' in sport. In cricket a batsman dismissed without scoring any runs is said to be **out for nought**, otherwise known as a **duck**. Originally the term was a **duck's egg**, from the shape of the numeral 0 next to the batsman's name on the scorecard. For the same reason, Americans use the informal expression **goose egg**. There is a popular belief that the tennis term **love** has a similar origin, a corruption of *l'oeuf*, the French for 'egg', though it seems more likely that it derives from the phrase 'play for love' (that is, for nothing). A 6–0 set in which one player fails to win a single game is colloquially known as a **bagel**, again from the round shape of the zero. A team failing to score a goal in football gets **nil** (a contraction of Latin *nihil*). Sometimes **nothing** is used, especially among Scottish football managers, as in 'we won two nothing'. A 0–0 scoreline is usually given in speech as **nil-nil**, though **nil-all** and **none-none** are common alternatives. Such a draw is usually described as **goalless** or, less logically, **scoreless**.

None (or **no wicket**) is used in cricket to say that a team hasn't lost any wickets, as in '42 for none'. A euphemistic phrase for being dismissed for a duck is **failing to trouble the scorers**. A batsman scoring nought twice in the same match gets a **pair** (short for **pair of spectacles**). **Zero** isn't used much in giving scorelines. Its main sporting use is in the phrase 'from hero to zero', when a previously idolized player falls from grace.

Ball of the Century

For cricket fans, the undisputed **Ball of the Century** was the sensational delivery bowled by Australian spinner Shane Warne to dismiss English batsman Mike Gatting on 4 June 1993, at Old Trafford, Manchester. Warne's arrival into Ashes cricket had been eagerly anticipated, and this was his very first ball in a Test match in England. The ball pitched outside leg stump, spun prodigiously round Gatting's legs after bouncing, completely bamboozling the batsman and clipping the top of his off stump.

ballpark figure

Why is a **ballpark figure** an approximate one, a rough estimate? This figurative usage, dating from the 1950s, comes from the idea that a ballpark – a baseball ground – is a large space rather than a precisely defined spot. *See also* IN THE RIGHT BALLPARK.

ball-watching

Keeping your eye on the ball would seem to be a laudable activity for a footballer but a player, especially a defender, is deemed to be guilty of **ball-watching** when his eyes are glued to the movement of the ball and he has utterly failed to notice where the opposing players have got to, allowing one or more of them to get into an advantageous position:

United were caught ball-watching and gave Carl Baker the space to tap home. cambridge-news.co.uk, 3/10/05

See also TAKE YOUR EYE OFF THE BALL.

bandbox

A small baseball park, favoured by batters because of the ease of hitting the ball beyond the outfield fence and score a home run, is sometimes described as a **bandbox**, from the lightweight box used for holding hats and other articles of clothing.

● banjo hitter

Banjo hitter is a disparaging baseball term for a weak-hitting batter, who hits mostly singles over a short distance. The bat supposedly makes contact with the ball with the sound of a twanging banjo.

● baseliner

Baseliners are tennis players who rarely stray from the baseline (the chalk line at the far end of the court) during a rally.

● basket

Just as in football a goal is both the frame for the net and the point you score for getting the ball into it, so in basketball the term **basket** is used both for the high hoop and net and for the act of scoring a point: 'A last-second basket by Kobe Bryant gave the Lakers a dramatic win.' Suspended peach baskets were originally used when the sport was invented in the 1890s, which is why it is called basketball.

● bat for

In American English, to **bat for** someone or something (or **go out to bat for** them) is to support or defend them, as in the headline 'Former Senator John Glenn Goes to Bat for Democrats'. The expression derives from baseball.

● batter

Batters play baseball and batsmen play cricket. Simple, eh? Well, not quite. In cricket the use of the term **batter** to describe a cricketer who is batting or is a specialist at batting (once more common than 'batsman' but displaced by the latter term in the mid-19th century) is now largely restricted to the context of women's cricket, as a gender-neutral alternative to 'batswoman'. It is also sometimes used by Australians. There is evidence,

though, that 'batter' is enjoying something of a more widespread
revival both among journalists and players:

*As a batter obviously you would want to spend some time in the
middle and I am happy that I got to spend some time out there.*
Shivnarine Chanderpaul, 14/11/05

*We claimed twenty wickets in the first Test but our batters didn't apply
themselves enough in these conditions to get the big scores and put
them under enough pressure.*   Michael Vaughan, 3/12/05

● Battle of the Long Count

On 22 September 1927, Jack Dempsey and Gene Tunney contested
the world heavyweight title. In the seventh round, Dempsey
knocked Tunney to the floor, but the former's failure to retire to a
neutral corner caused the referee to delay starting the count. The
resulting 'long count' of at least 14 seconds may have been crucial
in giving Tunney time to recover and he went on to win the fight.
This contest was subsequently dubbed the **Battle of the Long
Count**. *See also* RUMBLE IN THE JUNGLE, THRILLA IN MANILA.

● beat the gun

A sprinter who **beats the gun** leaves the starting blocks before
the sound of the starting pistol. *See also* B OF THE BANG.

● beautiful game

Journalists sometimes refer to football as the **beautiful game**,
especially the free-flowing variety full of artistry and skill played
by Brazil. Indeed, the phrase is attributed to the Brazilian
footballer Pelé, whose 1977 autobiography had the title *My Life
and the Beautiful Game*. It is often used in headlines such as 'The
Ugly Side of the Beautiful Game'.

● bed and breakfast

In cricket, a **bed-and-breakfast pitch** is a benign pitch that is very good for batting on, so called because the batsman can metaphorically book himself in overnight and still expect to be there the following day: 'He looks like he's booking himself in for bed and breakfast.' The term **bed and breakfast** also crops up in darts, where it denotes a score of 26, the total score after hitting 20 and, on either side of it on the board, 5 and 1. The expression comes from 'two and six' (that is, two shillings and sixpence), at one time the typical cost of bed and breakfast.

● behind the eight ball

To be **behind the eight ball** is to be in a highly difficult or awkward position from which it is difficult to extricate yourself. The expression comes from a variety of the game of pool, called eight-ball pool. The black ball, marked with the number 8, mustn't be pocketed until the end, so if it is blocking your path to any other ball, there is a danger of you pocketing the black ball and losing the game. Both the situation and the figurative extension resemble 'snookered'.

● below the belt

The phrase **below the belt**, describing a remark that is unfair or cruel, originally comes from boxing. It is against the rules for a boxer to land a blow below the level of his opponent's navel-high waistband.

● bench

In the context of a football match, the **bench** is the area to the side of the pitch where the manager, coaching staff and substitutes sit, just near the touchline. The word can be applied not only to the location but to the people themselves, as in 'the Arsenal bench are not happy'. Linguistically speaking, the use of 'the bench' here is an example of the figure of speech called metonymy, where a word or expression that refers to an attribute of something is substituted for the thing itself. So 'the crown' can be used to refer to a monarch and indeed 'the bench' can also refer to the magistrates or judges sitting in a court. A player is said to be **on the bench** (or to be **benched**) when he is named as a substitute, not as a member of the starting eleven.

● bench warmer

Benches play a significant part in the lexicon of substitutes. In American sport, a **bench warmer** is a substitute who gets few opportunities to play: 'He went from a bench warmer to a full-time starter in his first season.' A player may spend most of a season 'warming the bench'. *See also* BENCH, RIDE THE PINE.

● between the sticks

Between the sticks is a slightly arch journalistic expression meaning 'between the goalposts', the domain of the goalkeeper. A goalkeeper might be described as 'a dominant presence between the sticks' or applauded for 'a fine performance between the sticks'.

● big ask

Originally an Australian usage, but currently widespread in British sport, a **big ask** is a difficult target or demand, a real challenge, a tall order. In meaning the expression matches 'it's asking a lot'. The use of 'ask' as a noun here is interesting linguistically, analogous to expressions like 'a good read' or (of a radio programme) 'an enjoyable listen'. Asks of a greater magnitude than big can be described as 'huge' or even 'massive'.

We've got to try to get into the top six. It's a big ask but I don't think it's beyond this team. Alan Shearer, Newcastle United, 2/2/2005

We've not actually beaten Argentina for 15 years, are behind them in the world rankings and they've taken some mighty scalps recently, so we

go into Saturday's game as the underdogs. It's a huge ask but we're finally turning the corner and feel we can pull it off. Chris Cusiter, Scotland scrum-half, 11/11/2005
See also MOUNTAIN TO CLIMB.

● big boys

'Now we've gone up to play with the big boys, we're finding the going a little harder this year': newly promoted teams who find themselves facing opposition at a higher level than they have been accustomed to are said to be **playing** (or **mixing it**) **with the big boys**. It is an expression with a touch of the school playground about it. In tournaments or cup competitions, too, a lowly team (often described as a 'minnow') might find itself drawn against one of the big boys.

● big serve

In the language of tennis, a **big serve** is a fast serve with a lot of power: 'Roddick has a big serve.'

● birdcage

In American football, a **birdcage** is an informal name for the protective facemask with additional vertical and horizontal bars worn by linemen (the players who line up on the line of scrimmage).

● birdie

A **birdie** is a hole at golf completed with a score of one stroke under par. According to golf folklore the origin of the term goes back to a game played in 1903 in Atlantic City in the US. A shot that enabled a player called Ab Smith to take a stroke less than par on a hole was greeted with the words 'That's a bird of a shot!' 'Bird' was a slang term for anything excellent, dating back to the 19th century. **Birdie** can also be used as a verb: 'Garcia birdied the 9th.' *See also* ALBATROSS, EAGLE.

bird's nest

There are a number of colourful expressions to describe the
position from which a golf ball has to be played (the lie),
particularly when it is resting in an awkward spot. If the ball is
embedded in deep grass, the top just peeping out like an egg in a
nest, the lie can be referred to as a **bird's nest**. *See also* FRIED EGG.

bits-and-pieces player

Bits-and-pieces player is a mildly disparaging term for a
cricketer who can make contributions with both bat and ball but
is not a specialist in either discipline: 'He has progressed from
being a bits-and-pieces player to a genuine all-rounder.' The term
is mainly used in the context of one-day cricket. Such a player is
also known as a 'utility player'.

bleachers

To non-Americans, the line 'I go to ballgames, the bleachers are
fine', from the Rodgers and Hart song 'The Lady is a Tramp', may
be slightly baffling. The **bleachers** are the inexpensive bench
seats in the uncovered section of a sports ground. Because the
seats are not covered, the sun bleaches them.

bleeder

A boxer who is susceptible to being cut by an opponent's punches
is known in boxing circles as a **bleeder**.

blitz

A **blitz** is a manoeuvre in American football in which players
of the defensive team (linebackers and defensive backs, whose
position is normally behind the line of scrimmage) charge
forwards towards the opposing line of players in an attempt
to tackle the opposing quarterback or force him to make a
hurried pass.

● blockhole

In cricket, the **blockhole** is the spot on the crease between where the batsman rests the end of his bat while waiting to receive a ball and his toes. A delivery that pitches here, 'in the blockhole', can be difficult for the batsman to keep out. *See also* YORKER.

● blood bin

The grisly-sounding **blood bin** is where a rugby player is sent to have a bleeding wound treated before he can come back onto the pitch.

● bloop

In baseball, a **bloop** (or **blooper**) is a softly hit ball, especially a mishit, which lands just beyond the infield.

● blot on the handicap

A racehorse that 'looks like' (or 'could prove to be') a **blot on the handicap** is one whose ability appears to have been underestimated by the handicapper and has as a result been allocated less weight than its past performances would seem to merit. *See also* HANDICAP SNIP.

● blow up

In the language of horse racing, a horse **blows up** when it suddenly drops out of contention in the final stages of a race, usually because of exhaustion:

He made some very eye-catching progress about six furlongs out but then just blew up towards the finish. normileracing.co.uk, 19/11/05

When You Sir made his debut at Punchestown in November he led the field until he blew up in the straight. Kilkenny People, 9/7/05

board

A **board** in basketball is a rebound, bouncing off the backboards (sometimes called the boards) above the basket.

body blow

A deeply felt shock, disappointment or setback is sometimes referred to as a **body blow**. The expression comes from boxing, in which it describes a heavy punch to the body.

B of the Bang

Olympic sprinter Linford Christie used to say that he left the starting blocks not merely at the 'bang' of the starting pistol, but at the **B of the Bang**, vividly suggesting the speed of his reactions and the explosiveness of his start. The phrase inspired, and is the title of, a huge, spiky, starburst-like sculpture constructed outside the City of Manchester Stadium to commemorate the 2002 Commonwealth Games held in that city. The tallest self-supporting sculpture in the UK, it was designed by Thomas Heatherwick.

bogey

Nowadays a **bogey** is a hole at golf completed with a score of one stroke over par. The word originally meant the number of strokes a good player was expected to need to complete a course or a single hole. In US usage this was often one stroke above par and this is what the word came to mean. The word dates back to the 1890s and probably derives from the old word *bogey*, meaning the Devil or an evil spirit, perhaps because golfers imagined this standard score was a mischievously tricky opponent they were competing against. **Bogey** can also be used as a verb, as in 'she bogeyed the 12th'. To 'play bogey golf' is to average a bogey on every hole.

● bomb

A **bomb** is a long pass thrown downfield by a quarterback to a receiver.

● bonk

For those unfamiliar with cycling jargon, the connection between the word **bonk** and sport is probably limited to the nickname Bonking Boris. The German tennis player Boris Becker was so dubbed by the British tabloids because he was supposed to have attributed his loss of form during the 1987 Wimbledon championship to having had too much sex. **Bonking** in cycling, however, is much less rude. The term describes the sudden and complete exhaustion and loss of energy a rider can experience during a long day's racing if he has not taken in enough food or liquid. It is the cyclist's equivalent of 'hitting the wall'. *See also* HIT THE WALL.

● bootleg

There is a manoeuvre in American football in which a quarterback pretends to transfer the ball to a teammate running in one direction while the quarterback himself hides the ball behind his hip and runs in the opposite direction. This piece of misdirection is known as a **bootleg**. In the 19th century bootleggers were smugglers (so called because they originally carried bottles of liquor concealed in their boots) and the quarterback may be thought of as smuggling the ball in a similarly cunning way:

Roethlisberger scored Pittsburgh's first touchdown on a bootleg.
stltoday.com, 5/2/06

● bore draw

A woefully dull football match that ends 0–0 often attracts the dismissive, albeit rhyming, description of **bore draw**, especially in newspaper headlines: 'Boro and Charlton in FA Cup Bore Draw'.

● bosie

Bosie is a cricketing term formerly used in Australia for what is more widely known as a 'googly'. The word is derived from the name of the English spin bowler B. J. T. Bosanquet, who invented this type of delivery in the early 1900s and had great success with it when bowling for the MCC on the 1903–4 tour of Australia. *See also* GOOGLY.

● Bosman

The Belgian player Jean-Marc Bosman is one of the few footballers whose name has entered the dictionary. The so-called 'Bosman ruling' allows professional footballers in the EU to leave their club when their contract expires and move to another club on a free transfer. When Bosman was refused permission to move from the Belgian club Liège to the French club Dunkerque once his contract expired in 1990, the player took his case for restraint of trade to the European Court of Justice, a case he won in 1995. The Court found that the existing transfer rules breached EU law on free movement of workers between member states. The phrases **do a Bosman** and **leave on a Bosman**, meaning 'leave at the end of a contract on a free transfer', have now become part of the footballing lexicon. *See also* CURT FLOOD CASE.

● boss the game

Used particularly in football and rugby, the expression **boss the game** means to dominate or control it. Teams can be said to boss the game when they outplay their opponents and the phrase can also be applied to an individual player whose commanding presence on the pitch exerts an influence over the whole course of a match. In football the term tends to be used of 'playmaking' midfielders.

● bouncebackability

Iain Dowie, the former manager of Crystal Palace football club (2003–6), has the distinction of coining a new word that has found its way into dictionaries. It's not often that you can identify an individual directly responsible for a new coinage, but with **bouncebackability** you can. In a post-match press conference in 2004, Dowie credited his team, who had equalized against Arsenal, with showing 'great bouncebackability', that is, a capacity to recover quickly from a setback. So delighted with this new word were the presenters of the Sky TV programme *Soccer AM* that they campaigned to get it into the dictionary. 'Bouncebackability' duly appeared as an entry in the 2005 edition of the *Collins English Dictionary*.

● box clever

In British English, to **box clever** is to act in a clever or cunning way to get what you want, like an experienced boxer who outwits his opponent in the ring.

● box-to-box

Where the similar expression 'end-to-end' is used to describe an exciting football game with plenty of goalmouth incident at both ends of the pitch, **box-to-box** tends to be applied to an individual player, usually an industrious midfielder who spends a game tirelessly running up and down the pitch (between his team's penalty box and the opposing team's one) to perform both defensive and attacking duties. *See also* END-TO-END.

● bragging rights

In a derby game, **bragging rights** (the right of the winning team and its supporters to gloat) are said to be at stake. They can be won, earned, claimed, secured, retained, enjoyed or lost: 'Arsenal claim local bragging rights over Chelsea', 'the blue half of Manchester are enjoying the bragging rights tonight'.

breadstick

A set in tennis won 6–0 is known as a **bagel** because of the resemblance between the shape of a zero and that of a bagel. Continuing the bakery theme, a set won 6–1 is a **breadstick**.

break

In tennis, if your opponent wins a game when they are receiving and you are serving, they have **broken** your serve (and you have suffered a **break**). If you immediately go on to win the next game, when your opponent is the one serving, you have **broken back**.

break your duck

In cricket, to **break your duck** is to score the first runs of your innings, to 'get off the mark'. Figuratively, **breaking your duck** is achieving a success for the first time after several failures. *See also* DUCK.

brick

Bricks aren't known for their aerodynamic properties and in basketball a **brick** is a hard, poorly directed shot that easily misses the basket and bounces wildly off the rim or backboard. Players badly off-target are said to 'shoot' or 'throw' bricks.

broom wagon

Football has its sweepers and cycle racing has its broom wagon. In the Tour de France, the **broom wagon** (*voiture balai* in French) is a support vehicle that travels behind the backmarkers and picks up any riders who have had to abandon the race because of fatigue or injury.

bucket

The basket in basketball is colloquially known as the **bucket**, and, like **basket**, the word can also be used to mean the act of scoring:

A bucket by Tina Thompson cut the lead to 6. nwbl.com, 25/1/04

● buffet bowling

Buffet bowling in cricket is poor-quality bowling that is so innocuous that batsmen 'can help themselves' to runs: 'The England bowlers served up too much buffet bowling in the morning session and the Australian batsmen tucked in.' An alternative term is 'cafeteria bowling'. *See also* PIE CHUCKER.

● bullocking

In rugby, the adjective **bullocking** (Australian in origin) is habitually used to describe a powerful run by a strongly built player, bursting through the opponents' defence. The word suggests a one-man stampede:

Stung by the set-back, Wasps hit back almost immediately thanks to a bullocking run from wing Rudd that sucked in the Ponty defenders. bbc.co.uk, 12/4/03

● bullpen

The **bullpen** is the fenced-in area of a baseball ground where the pitchers warm up before they start pitching. The word is also used for a baseball team's relief pitchers. These baseball uses probably derive from an older meaning of *bullpen*, a large cell where prisoners awaiting trial are detained before appearing in court.

● bump and run

A golfer who 'plays a lot of **bump and run**' favours approach shots hit so that the ball lands short of the green and then rolls a long distance up onto the green: 'He hit a bump-and-run shot that stopped two feet from the hole.'

● bunny

In cricket, if a particular batsman is prone to getting out to the same bowler, he can be described as that bowler's **bunny**. Michael Atherton was said to be Glenn McGrath's bunny, the Australian fast bowler dismissing him a total of nineteen times in Test

As the end of the football season approaches, teams near the foot of the table (the **basement**) and in danger of being relegated to the division below are said to be in the **relegation zone**, also known as the **drop zone**.

Much of the language associated with relegation relates to the idea of falling, dropping or sinking, with trapdoors and quicksand providing useful metaphors.

These anxious teams are **facing the drop** and trying to avoid falling through the relegation **trapdoor**. **Dragged** (or **sucked**) into a relegation **dogfight** with the **fellow-strugglers** around them, their aim is to **stay up** rather than **go down**.

Those short of points with only a few games left find themselves **deep in the relegation mire** and striving to 'drag' themselves 'out' of it. Whether a team **avoids the drop** may only be decided on the last day of the season: it may go right **down to the wire**.

RELEGATION

matches. Adam Gilchrist was described as Andrew Flintoff's bunny after being dismissed on four occasions by the bowler during the 2005 Ashes series. The word **bunny** can also be used to mean a very poor batsman, one of the tailenders, although the more common term is 'rabbit'. In basketball, a **bunny** is a very easy shot, under no challenge from the defending players. *See also* RABBIT.

● bunsen

The cricketing term **bunsen** is short for bunsen burner, which is rhyming slang for turner. And what is a turner? It's a turning wicket, that is, a wicket on which a spin bowler can make the ball deviate a long way after bouncing. A particularly spin-friendly wicket is sometimes described as 'a raging bunsen'.

It's hard to see them beating Warne and Stuart MacGill on a 'bunsen' in the Sydney cauldron. Scotland on Sunday, 3/11/02

● bunt

A **bunt** is a baseball term for when a batter deliberately hits the ball gently without swinging the bat but merely letting the ball hit it, allowing the batter to place the ball a short distance beyond the infield so that a runner is able to advance. Batters 'lay down' or 'drop down' a bunt. It is the equivalent of playing the ball with a 'dead bat' in cricket.

● buy a goal

It is said, often sympathetically, of an out-of-form (or unlucky) striker who hasn't scored for a long time that 'he **can't buy a goal**'. The opposite is 'he scores goals **for fun**'. The expression is used of teams too: 'We're creating enough chances but we just can't buy a goal at the moment.' Similarly, a struggling basketball player 'can't buy a basket'. In darts, the expression 'can't buy a double' is sometimes heard. *See also* GOAL DROUGHT, SELL A DUMMY.

● buy a wicket

Buying a wicket is a cricketing term describing bowling and fielding tactics that are designed to encourage the batsman to hit attacking shots and score quick runs in the hope that he will be tempted to play a reckless shot along the way and thus get out:

Hussain brought on part-time off-spinner Ramprakash in a desperate bid to buy a wicket. thatscricket.oneindia.in, 17/8/01

The 'cost' of the desired wicket is the potentially large number of runs that the bowler may concede. The expression **can't buy a wicket** can be used with a different meaning, analogous to **can't buy a goal** in football. A bowler who can't buy a wicket seems unable to take a wicket whatever efforts they make or stratagems they use:

Ashley Giles could hardly buy a wicket in Bangladesh. cricinfo.com, 19/8/04

c

call a cab

A jockey is said to be **calling a cab** when he puts an arm in the air to try to keep his balance after a mistake in jumping a fence, supposedly resembling someone hailing a taxi.

call the shots

The person who **calls the shots** in a situation is in control and makes the important decisions. The phrase is borrowed from the game of pool, in which a player is required to announce in advance of playing a shot which ball he intends to hit into which pocket.

can of corn

Can of corn is the baseball equivalent of the cricket term **dolly**, that is, an easy catch for a fielder: 'That was a can of corn and he dropped it.' It is thought that the expression derives from the idea of a general store clerk reaching up to a high shelf and knocking a can down into his hands. More generally, Americans use the phrase to mean anything easily accomplished, a cinch, 'a piece of cake'.

canvas

The floor of the boxing ring is called the **canvas**, from the stretched canvas that covers it. A boxer who is knocked down by his opponent is commonly said to 'hit the canvas', to be 'sent to the canvas', or to be 'put on the canvas'. In rowing, the **canvas** is the covered foredeck of a boat and the term is used to describe the margin of victory in a close race, a maximum of six feet: 'In 1980 Oxford won by a canvas.' *See also* HEAD, LENGTH, NOSE.

card

In golf, you can talk about **carding** a particular score for a round of golf or a hole, as in 'Woods carded a final-round 69' or 'she carded birdies on the 10th and 11th to get to three under'. This is because you actually write down your hole-by-hole score on a scorecard as you play a round of golf.

carry the drinks

Although there is more to the duties of being a twelfth man (as the reserve member of a cricket side is called) than taking the drinks out to the other players on the pitch during drinks breaks, the term **carry the drinks** can simply mean 'be the twelfth man':

Brad Williams will probably come into the XI for the Test in place of Gillespie, with Bracken likely to carry the drinks. fs.cricket365.com, 14/10/03

The term 'drinks waiter' is also used, as in 'Lee is likely to keep his role as drinks waiter for the second Test'.

carry your bat

To **carry your bat** in cricket is to bat all the way through your side's innings without losing your wicket, in other words to be one of the opening batsmen and to remain not out when the other ten wickets have fallen:

Gavaskar carried his bat through the Indian second innings scoring a magnificent 127. cricketzone.com, 5/3/05

● cart

In cricket, to **cart** the ball is to hit it very hard and high in the air:

The Lancashire all-rounder carted the ball to all parts of the ground. bbc.co.uk, 8/8/05

The word is used in other sports, particularly rugby, to describe kicking the ball powerfully and unceremoniously upfield or away from a dangerous position.

● castle

A batsman is **castled** in cricket when he is bowled and some of the stumps are dislodged. The word comes from a former use of **castle** to refer to the stumps that the batsman is defending against attack.

● catch a crab

It's the piece of rowing jargon that everyone seems to know. When a rower **catches a crab** he either gets the oar caught under the surface of the water and can't lift it clear at the end of the stroke or misses the water altogether with the stroke. As a result the boat slows down and the oar handle may push the rower flat on his back or even throw him out of the boat. The phrase comes from the idea that the claws of a large crab have grabbed the oar.

● catch pigeons

Racehorses running impressively in training are claimed by their trainers to be **catching pigeons** 'at home' or 'on the gallops':

Balmont has reportedly been catching pigeons on Newmarket's plentiful gallops. sahorseracing.com, 12/10/04

Sport seems to revel in such ornithological metaphors. *See also*
ALBATROSS, DUCK, DUCKS ON THE POND, DYING QUAIL, EAGLE, GOOSE EGG,
QUAIL HIGH.

● caught in possession

To be **caught in possession** on a football pitch is to lose the ball
to a player from the opposing team:

*Hleb dribbles the ball dangerously in his own penalty area and almost
gets caught in possession before he finally makes the clearance.*
sportinglife.com, 28/1/06

It's a phrase that might in a different context suggest a raid by
the drug squad.

● centurion

In cricket, a **centurion** is a batsman who has scored a century, a
grander-sounding journalistic alternative to 'century-maker':

*Australia suffered an early setback when first-innings centurion Justin
Langer was caught behind off Ajit Agarkar for a duck.* bbc.co.uk, 8/12/03

*England recovered their composure after a merciless mauling at the
hands of double-centurion Mohammad Yousuf.*
www.manchesteronline.co.uk, 2/12/05

● chain gang

In American football, the **chain gang** (or **chain crew**) are the
group of officials whose job is to handle the 10-yard chain used
to measure how far a team has advanced the ball.

● chalk

Chalk plays a big part in tennis, at least on grass courts, because
of the importance of establishing whether a shot has bounced
inside or outside the white lines marking the boundaries of the

court. Players are often heard protesting that there was 'a puff of chalk', indicating that the ball landed on the line and was therefore in. The most famous example was John McEnroe's outburst at Wimbledon in 1981: 'You cannot be serious! The ball was on the line! Chalk flew up!' A footballer who spends most of the game charging up the wing, hugging the touchline, is sometimes said to 'have chalk on his boots'. *See also* YOU CANNOT BE SERIOUS.

● chalk jockey

A **chalk jockey** is an inexperienced jockey. The term comes from pre-computerization days when riders' names at racecourses were printed on wooden boards. Those jockeys who hadn't yet had enough rides to warrant a printed board of their own had their names chalked onto a blank board instead.

● champagne

In the context of a football match, **champagne** suggests luxury and extravagance rather than celebration. A **champagne ball** is an over-elaborate or overambitious pass or cross, while a **champagne player** is one with too many flamboyant tricks. *See also* FANCY DAN, SHOWBOATING, SHOW PONY.

● chanceless

A **chanceless** innings made by a batsman in a cricket match is one that offers no opportunity for the fielding side to get him out. By 'chances' is usually meant catches that go to hand and are dropped or plausible LBW appeals. The word *chanceless* is uncommon in contexts outside cricket.

● charity stripe

The free-throw line on a basketball court is informally known as the **charity stripe**, a term coined by the US broadcaster Chick Hearn.

cheaply

One of the cardinal sins on a football pitch is to 'give the ball away **cheaply**', that is, to lose possession of the ball unnecessarily because of a misplaced pass when under little pressure from the opposing team. A team may 'pay dearly' for giving the ball away cheaply, or it may 'cost them'. Other commerce-related pieces of football phraseology include **can't buy a goal** and **sell a dummy**. In cricket, a bowler removes a batsman **cheaply** when he gets the batsman out for a low score.

cheap shot

In American football, a **cheap shot** is a deliberate foul on an unsuspecting opposing player, especially one from behind. In extended use, the term is used to refer to a remark or criticism that takes unfair advantage of someone.

cheap yards

In sports such as rugby and American football, **cheap yards** are those gains in territory with the ball that are achieved with the minimum of effort, because the tackling from the opposing team is so ineffectual:

This is a team that struggles to score and relies on defense, so it can't afford to give up cheap yards on kickoffs. Sporting News, 16/9/05

checkout

A **checkout** in darts is a score a player throws to win a game in one turn, as in 'a 118 checkout' or 'he played down to 52 but missed the checkout'.

cheese

Cheese is a rather curious piece of baseball slang, meaning a pitcher's fastball. *See also* HIGH CHEESE.

● cherry

A **cherry** is, in cricketers' slang, a cricket ball, red and shiny, especially in the phrase 'new cherry' or 'shiny cherry'. The expression 'new nut' is also used.

● chicane

A **chicane** is a short section of tight turns in alternate directions on a motor-racing circuit, intended to force drivers to reduce their speed. The word originally meant 'chicanery or trickery'.

● chin

A boxer's **chin** is his ability to take hard punches to the head without being knocked out, as in 'he is strong and has a pretty good chin' or 'a boxer with a good punch but no chin'. *See also* GLASS JAW.

● chinaman

The cricketing term **chinaman** is generally taken to refer to a delivery bowled by a left-arm wrist spinner that moves after pitching from the off side to the leg side, when bowling to a right-handed batsman. However, in Australian usage, and rather confusingly, a **chinaman** is a ball that moves precisely the opposite way, from leg to off, and thus denotes the left-arm wrist spinner's 'googly'. The term is said to derive from the Trinidadian bowler Ellis 'Puss' Achong, who was of Chinese descent. *See also* GOOGLY.

● Chinese cut

A **Chinese cut** in cricket is an unintentional batting stroke where the ball is deflected off the inside edge of the bat and just misses the leg stump. Why Chinese? Probably from the former use of the word, based on a racist stereotype, to describe something devious or mystifying. The terms 'French cut' (likewise reflecting cultural stereotyping) and 'Surrey cut' are also used.

● Chinese snooker

In the game of snooker, a **Chinese snooker** is a position in which there is another ball immediately behind the cue ball (the ball you are trying to hit with the cue), making it difficult to play the shot you want.

● chin music

'The openers had to face a few overs of chin music before the close': originating in the West Indies, the colloquial cricketing term **chin music** aptly describes fast, short-pitched bowling that is aimed at the batsman at around head height, such as was the stock-in-trade of the West Indian fast bowlers during their team's years of domination of Test cricket between the mid-1970s and the mid-1990s. In baseball, **chin music** refers to a series of pitches thrown close to a batter's head and intended to unsettle the batter. In American English, **chin music** can also be used as a slang expression meaning 'talk or chatter'. *See also* THROAT BALL.

● chip and charge

Like **give and go**, **hands and heels** and **truck and trailer**, **chip and charge** is one of those appealingly alliterative expressions popular with sportspeople. It describes an aggressive playing style in tennis, in which a player returns the opposing player's serve, giving the ball a lot of backspin, and rushes forward to the net:

My game plan was to chip and charge and get into the net. Leander Paes, 20/8/98

See also SERVE AND VOLLEY.

● choke

It is sometimes said that professional sport at the highest level is to a large extent played in the mind, and this is never better demonstrated than when a competitor appears to **choke** when the prize of victory is within his or her grasp. **Choking** is losing your composure in a high-pressure situation when seemingly in a winning position, with the result that your game completely falls apart. Among many famous sporting contests that are often cited as examples of such a mental collapse are Jana Novotna's failure to win the 1993 Wimbledon final (when leading Steffi Graf 4–1 and 40–30 in the third set) and the traumatic implosion of Greg Norman's game on the final day of the 1996 US Masters. **Choker** is a label that no sportsman or sportswoman wants to be saddled with, the ultimate insult, akin to a soldier being branded a coward.

● chucker

In cricketing slang, a **chucker** is a bowler suspected of 'throwing', that is, bowling with an illegal action in which the elbow is straightened during a delivery. *See also* THROWING.

● class

Sportsmen and women who display stylish excellence are praised for their **class**, as in 'Thierry Henry just oozes class', 'Lara is a class player' or 'Safin is clearly a class act'. As with 'quality', adjectives like 'high' and 'top' are understood. *See also* DIFFERENT CLASS, QUALITY.

● clean air

In motor racing, air can be described as either clean or dirty and it has nothing to do with exhaust fumes. **Clean air** is air free of turbulence, enjoyed by a car not following closely behind another car, for example because it is leading the race. *See also* DIRTY AIR.

● clean sheet

Goalkeepers and defenders pride themselves on 'keeping a **clean sheet**', that is, not conceding a goal. Sheet here means scoresheet. The equivalent term in US sport is 'posting' a **shutout**. *See also* SHUTOUT.

● clean the glass

A basketball player who is a good rebounder (that is, who is skilled at catching the ball as it bounces off the glass backboard and whipping it into the basket) will often be praised for his ability to **clean the glass**. An extension of this idea is to refer to the proprietary glass cleaner Windex, as in 'Brown cleaned more glass than Windex' or 'he's the team's Windex man'.

● clear the table

In snooker, a player **clears the table** by successfully pocketing all the balls remaining on the table, ending with the black. This is called a **clearance**. *See also* TABLE SETTER.

● clever feet

It is common for human attributes to be ascribed to parts of the body. For example, footballers' feet can be described as 'cultured' and 'educated'. And they can be **clever**: 'The Dutchman has clever feet and great pace.' *See also* DESPAIRING HANDS.

● cleverly

In horse-racing jargon, a horse that wins a race **cleverly** does so more easily than the winning distance might suggest:

Godolphin's Fantastic Light landed the Group 1 Tattersalls Gold Cup, winning cleverly by a neck from Golden Snake. telegraph.co.uk, 27/5/01

● climb the ladder

Climbing the ladder, an expression used in American football, is jumping extremely high to catch the ball, as in 'his ability to climb the ladder and get up for high passes'.

● close the door

In motor racing and horse racing, to **close the door** (or **shut the door**) is to move over to prevent another competitor from finding a way through a gap as the finishing line approaches.

See also PUT UP THE SHUTTERS.

● clothesline

A **clothesline** (or **clothesline tackle**) in American football is the act of knocking down another player by striking them across the face or neck with an outstretched arm, as if they had run straight into a clothesline. A player felled in this way can be said to have been **clotheslined**.

● clutch

'Pirates Fail in the Clutch' ran a headline in a Pittsburgh newspaper in 2005. A key term in baseball, the **clutch** is a critical point in a game, 'the crunch'. A player who may be depended upon to put in a good performance under pressure at a crucial time may be described as 'coming through in the clutch' or as a **clutch player**. *See also* CHOKE, FLAT-TRACK BULLY.

● coast-to-coast

In basketball jargon, going **coast-to-coast** means taking the ball from one end of the basketball court to the other: 'He stole the ball and went coast-to-coast for an easy lay-up finish.'

● coffin corner

Coffin corner is a term used in American football. It refers to one of the four corners of the field into which the ball is often deliberately kicked so that it will go out of bounds close to the defending team's goal line, requiring them to put the ball back into play dangerously near their own end zone. There is little margin for error for the kicker. The term **coffin corner** is borrowed from aeronautics, where it refers to a point at which a particular combination of critical factors (such as speed, altitude and angle of flight) makes the aircraft unstable and impossible to fly.

● come again

In horse racing, to **come again** is to regain ground in a race having previously fallen back.

● come to the party

To **come to the party** is to put in a good performance for your team, especially after a previously disappointing contribution. The term is used only in team sports.

And when Stephen Harmison joined in with a probing spell, all the England fast men who were off the pace yesterday had come to the party today. Steven Lynch, cricinfo.com, 5/9/03

Mark Schwarzer... was nearly taken off before penalties, but came to the party big time with two stunning spot-kick saves to book a place in Germany. news.bbc.co.uk, 30/11/05

● comfort zone

Though the term **comfort zone**, a choice example of psychobabble, is by no means confined to the world of sport, its use among professional sportspeople is widespread. It can refer to a state of relative ease during a contest when a team or player appears to be coasting and is not being put under pressure:

As a coach, I'd be willing to give up 14 early points if we can get a quarterback out of his comfort zone for the rest of the game. Cellar Dweller, sportscolumn.com, 30/11/05

The term can also be used when admonishing those who avoid stretching or testing themselves or making a greater effort to improve:

India need to get out of their comfort zone and develop a better all-round game with bat and ball. Mark Waugh, Sydney Morning Herald, 7/11/04

See also DROP ZONE, IN THE ZONE.

● consolation

Commentators always describe a late goal scored by a team who are already too many goals down to have a chance of winning the game as a **consolation goal**. If the team hasn't played as badly as the margin of defeat would have suggested, the adjective 'deserved' is thrown in for good measure.

● corridor of uncertainty

The Corridor of Uncertainty wouldn't sound out of place in Bunyan's allegory *Pilgrim's Progress*, alongside the Slough of Despond and the Valley of Humiliation. In the language of cricket, the phrase **corridor of uncertainty** (sometimes simply **the corridor**) describes the narrow area on and just outside a bats-man's off stump. A ball delivered here by the bowler can leave the batsman unsure whether or not he should play a stroke. The expression may have first appeared in print in a piece by John Woodcock in *The Times* in 1986, but Geoffrey Boycott has since popularized it.

Bell edged one in the corridor of uncertainty that saw Gilchrist take a neat catch tumbling to his right. bbc.co.uk, 25/8/05

● cover all the bases

To **cover all the bases** is to consider and deal with every possibility when you are planning something. In baseball, where the expression originates, a fielder covers a base by running towards it to make himself available to receive a throw and prevent the runner from reaching it safely. *See also* GET TO FIRST BASE, OFF BASE, TOUCH BASE.

● cow corner

Cow corner is the area of a cricket ground in front of the
batsman on the leg side (more specifically, the area between deep
midwicket and long-on). It is so-called because batsmen, skilled
ones at least, do not aim to hit the ball in this region very much
and fielders are not usually placed there: cows could graze there
without fear of being hit. Cow corner is, appropriately, where
many an 'agricultural shot' ends up. *See also* AGRICULTURAL SHOT,
COW SHOT, HOT CORNER.

● cow shot

In cricket, a **cow shot** is an inelegant slog, lacking much
technique, towards the leg-side boundary, otherwise known as
cow corner.

● cox

The **cox** is the non-rowing member of the rowing crew who steers
the boat during a race and gives instructions to the rowers. Cox
is short for *coxswain*, originally spelt *cockswain* and ultimately
deriving from the old words *cock* (or *cockboat*), 'a small boat towed
behind a larger vessel', and *swain*, 'a young man or servant'.

● crash ball

In rugby, to pass the ball to another player, or receive a pass, on
the **crash ball** is to do so just as the player making the pass is
tackled:

*Michalak's reverse pass in midfield unleashed centre Damien Traille on
the crash ball and, with the Irish defence sucked in, Michalak and
Brusque handled swiftly to put Clerc over on the right touchline.*
www.rugby.ie, 14/2/04

IMMEDIATELY a match has finished, elated or downcast players, often physically and emotionally drained, step off the field of play. When confronted with an interviewer's microphone, it is not surprising that they often resort to somewhat formulaic turns of phrase.

POST-MATCH INTERVIEW

Players acknowledge their own team's poor performance (**bad day at the office**, **not at the races**) or a good performance by the opposition (**credit to them**). They explain that they needed to find reserves of stamina (**we had to dig deep**) or failed to do so (**we had nothing left in the tank**). Players and managers alike tend not to be triumphalist or gung-ho in victory. Reactions are more commonly characterized by a modest downplaying of one's own contribution in a team game (**main thing is we got the three points**, **all credit to the rest of the lads**), a cautious reluctance to make predictions about future success (the ubiquitous **we're taking one game at a time**, **it's a big ask**) or simply relief (**we're just glad to be still in the hat**). Defeat is routinely turned into an opportunity for positive thinking (**it's a wake-up call for us**, **we'll regroup and bounce back**). Indeed one of the statutory clichés of the post-defeat interview is **taking the positives** (that is, the plus points, or perhaps simply an upbeat word for 'consolation') out of a performance. Managers, for their part, praise the effort and commitment of their team (**the players showed a lot of character, I couldn't ask more from my players, they gave 110 per cent**). *See also* TENSES p.65

● crash of ash

In cricket, the **crash of ash** is the dreaded sound of the stumps (made of ash) being dislodged as a batsman is bowled. *See also* DEATH RATTLE.

● crash out

In journalistic usage, to **crash out** of a knockout tournament, particularly in tennis and football, is to be eliminated. Often used in headlines, the phrase certainly sounds more dramatic than 'go out' or 'be knocked out' and seems particularly apt when the elimination of the player or team is at an unexpectedly early stage.

Henman Crashes Out in First Round headline, January 2006

Manchester United crashed out of the Champions League as they lost to Benfica in Lisbon's Stadium of Light. bbc.co.uk, 7/12/05

● credit to

In the post-match interview, a generous acknowledgement of an admirable performance by one's own team or a teammate or, if feeling magnanimous in defeat, the opposition, is frequently introduced by the phrase **credit to**, often preceded by 'all' or 'full':

When you look at the position we were in, what we have done is just fantastic and all credit to the players. Harry Redknapp, relegation-avoiding Portsmouth football club manager, 30/4/06

We could have played better, we know that, but credit to Seville because they are a class side who deserved to win. Gareth Southgate, Middlesbrough footballer, 10/5/06

● cricket score

The hyperbolic expression **cricket score** is used by football and rugby commentators to describe a high-scoring game, particularly when one team is giving its opponents a drubbing. Cricket scores tend to be 'run up', 'rattled up' or 'racked up': 'With more precise finishing Arsenal could have run up a cricket score.'

● crooked number

A **crooked number** is any number greater than 1 put up on a baseball scoreboard to record the number of runs a team scores in an inning. While 1 is simply a straight line, all other numbers are thought of as having bends or curves in them when written down. Coaches and players talk about 'getting a crooked number on the board'.

We've had trouble putting any crooked number up there lately. To put two numbers up there in one inning, that's pretty good. Bob Melvin, Seattle Mariners manager, 30/8/03

● cross the white line

In sport the painted white line marking the perimeter of the pitch can also symbolize for a player a mental transition in which off-pitch preparation, training, bonhomie and friendship give way to the serious business of the sporting contest about to take place, during which each player must stand up and be counted. Accordingly, the phrase **crossing** (or **stepping over**) **the** (or **that**) **white line** has become almost a cliché of the pre-match interview, used by players in football, baseball, tennis and many other sports. There is also the idea of stepping into the gladiatorial arena.

Myself and my staff will give the players our ideas, but they are the ones that once they cross the white line must deliver. Steve Staunton, Republic of Ireland football manager, 28/2/06

● crowd catch

A **crowd catch** in cricket is an apparent catch by a fielder that prompts a roar from the crowd but turns out to be not a catch at all, usually because the ball has already bounced after the batsman has played the shot, either very close to the batsman or very close to the fielder. There doesn't appear to be a term for the other kind of 'crowd catch', when a spectator catches a six hit into the stands.

● cultured

A favourite term of approval in football is **cultured**, as in 'a cultured midfielder', 'a cultured left foot', 'to play cultured football'. Nothing to do with being well read or going to the theatre, the word suggests a high level of technical skill and a degree of unhurried finesse. Cricketers can be similarly praised for 'a display of cultured strokeplay' or for scoring 'a cultured 60'. *See also* EDUCATED.

● cup

Golfers often refer to the hole on a green as the **cup**: 'the ball rolled into the cup', 'his putt slid past the left edge of the cup', 'her shot found the bottom of the cup'. Strictly speaking, the cup is the plastic or metal casing that lines the inside of the hole, but the term is frequently used for the hole itself.

● cup of coffee

A minor-league baseball player who spends only a short time playing at the major-league level before returning to the minor leagues is said to have had a **cup of coffee**. In other words, he has not eaten the full meal:

I had a cup of coffee with no sugar in it. Rod Dedeaux, baseball coach, on playing two games for the 1935 Brooklyn Dodgers, the sum of his major-league career

● cuppy

The adjective **cuppy** (meaning cup-shaped) always occurs with the noun 'lie' and describes a golf ball sitting in a small depression: 'He found his ball in a nasty cuppy lie.' *See also* BIRD'S NEST, FRIED EGG.

● cup-tied

If a player plays in an early round of a knockout cup competition and is then transferred to another club, they are ineligible to play for their new club in subsequent rounds of the same competition in the same season. The player is said to be **cup-tied**.

● Curt Flood case

Curt Flood was the Bosman of baseball. Like the Belgian footballer, Flood went to court to fight for his right to be a free agent. At the end of the 1969 season his team the St Louis Cardinals traded him to the Philadelphia Phillies, a move Flood himself objected to. He sued Major League Baseball on the grounds that the so-called 'reserve clause', binding a player to the team he was signed to and giving him no right to challenge a decision to trade him, was illegal. Although Flood's case was not successful, it opened the door for the scrapping of the reserve clause and the introduction of free agency in 1976. *See also* BOSMAN.

● custodian

Custodian is a rather old-fashioned and literary synonym for goalkeeper:

Chelsea FC's giant custodian Petr Cech was in irresistible form during their UEFA Champions League campaign. uefa.com, 1/7/05

The more elaborate version **custodian of the uprights** is used only humorously nowadays.

● cut

In golf tournaments, the **cut** is the mechanism by which the number of competitors is reduced at the midway point, specifically the highest score that a player needs to have in order to be allowed to continue playing in the remainder of the tournament.

Those that achieve that score or lower have 'made the cut' and play on; those that don't have 'missed the cut' and are eliminated from the field. *See also* MAKE THE CUT.

● cut each other's throats

When two or more front runners strenuously contest the lead during a horse race, only to let another horse that has paced itself better go on to win, they are said, in a colourful piece of racing jargon, to have **cut each other's throats**.

● cut man

In boxing, a **cut man** is a boxer's ringside assistant whose job is to treat cuts and reduce swellings between rounds and generally patch up the boxer in time for the next round.

d

dance floor

Dance floor is golfing slang for a putting green, from the smooth flat grass there: 'It wasn't the best of shots but at least he put his ball on the dance floor.'

dawn patrol

Golfers who tee off early in the morning are known colloquially as the **dawn patrol**.

dead fish

Not to be confused with a **dying quail**, a **dead fish** is baseball slang for a pitch thrown with very little speed, intended to make the batter swing at the ball prematurely. Metaphorically, it is lifeless and just flopping over the plate.

death overs

The last few overs of a one-day cricket match are known as the **death overs**, as in the expression 'at the death'. These are the climactic overs of the match, when the batsmen are closing in on their target and the bowlers are striving to take wickets and restrict runs:

India could have scored more, but Pakistani pacers bowled well in the death overs, denying the batsmen the chances to score freely.
the7am.com, 19/4/06

A **death bowler** is one who is particularly skilled at bowling these last crucial overs.

death rattle

In cricket, the **death rattle** is the sound a batsman hears behind him as he is bowled and his stumps are dislodged. *See also* CRASH OF ASH.

derby

A **derby** is a football match or other sporting contest between two rival teams from the same city or area. The term may derive from the traditional Shrovetide football match that was once played every year between two parishes in the city of Derby. Famous football derbies include those played in Manchester, Glasgow and Liverpool. Some derbies are more local than others. For example, the 'South Coast derby' is the fixture between Portsmouth and Southampton, while the 'M1 derby' is contested between Watford and Luton.

despairing hands

Commentators are fond of ascribing human emotions to parts of the body. One such linguistic oddity is the phrase **despairing hands**. The hands inevitably belong to a goalkeeper at full stretch and are so described when a shot is driven 'beyond' or 'past' them into the goal. *See also* CLEVER FEET.

deuce

In the tennis scoring system, **deuce** is the score of 40–40, where one player needs to win two points in a row in order to win the game. The word derives from the French expression *à deux de jeu* (literally meaning 'at two to play'). In baseball, a **deuce** is another name for a curveball (a pitched ball with a curving trajectory), often signalled by the catcher holding down two fingers. The term is also used for a double play, a manoeuvre in which two opposing players are put out. *See also* THROW A CURVEBALL.

● diamond duck

A **diamond duck** is when a batsman is out for nought off the very first ball of a cricket match. The term is sometimes applied to a batsman getting out without facing a single ball, for example if he is run out. *See also* DUCK, GOLDEN DUCK.

● different class

Different class is football-speak for 'a cut above' or 'top drawer'. The expression is associated particularly with Ally McCoist, the former Rangers player, now a TV pundit:

Barry Ferguson does the same kind of job in the middle of the park but Prso is different class. Ally McCoist, Daily Record, 15/10/05

See also CLASS.

● dig deep

To **dig deep** is to find reserves of strength, determination and self-belief within yourself when you are in severe difficulties and defeat appears certain. Such displays of grit and fighting spirit are the lifeblood of competitive sport. The phrase is typical of the terse, macho language of the professional sportsman:

Defiant Liverpool Dig Deep to Set Up Chelsea Showdown headline, The Times, 14/4/05

With 20 minutes to go we were up against it. They scored a great attacking try and we started to miss a few tackles but we dug deep, the character of the team came out and we got a great win. Gordon Bulloch, British & Irish Lions midweek team captain, 5/7/05

dime defense

In American football, a defensive formation with one extra defensive back, making five in total, is known as a 'nickel defense' (a nickel being worth five cents). One with two extra players, making six in total, is known as a **dime defense**. A dime, of course, is the equivalent of two nickels. *See also* NICKEL DEFENSE.

dirt-tracker

When a rugby squad is on tour, the team of second-string players fielded for the midweek matches as opposed to the more prestigious Test matches is known as the **dirt-trackers**. The term was popularized during the 1993 British Lions tour of New Zealand. A dirt track is a course made of rolled cinders or soil used for motorcycle races or flat races.

dirty air

In the context of motor racing, **dirty air** is the turbulence that a car creates in its wake and that has an adverse effect on the aerodynamics of a car following closely behind. *See also* CLEAN AIR.

disappointed

When a striker misses an open goal or a goalkeeper fails to make what should be a routine save, football commentators are fond of the polite understatement 'he'll be **disappointed** with that'.

dish

In the language of basketball, to **dish** the ball (or **dish** it **off**) is to pass it to a teammate:

After two timeouts, James dished the ball off to Donyell Marshall at the left corner and his three-point attempt rattled off the rim with 12.6 seconds left. baltimoresun.com, 22/3/06

In baseball, the plate (the home plate, over which the pitcher throws the ball) is sometimes referred to informally as the **dish**:

However, O'Day uncorked an errant throw into center field that allowed Grosse to cross the dish with the eventual winning run. gatorzone.com, 12/2/05

● DNF

One of the least desirable abbreviations in sport, **DNF** stands for 'did not finish', indicating that a competitor failed to complete the course in a race. *See also* MVP.

● do a bit

Cricketers use the phrase **do a bit** to suggest that the pitch is likely to be helpful to bowlers and to produce some unpredictable bounce and movement of the ball: 'the pitch did a bit this morning', 'the odd ball did a bit'.

● dodgy keeper

The football fans' adjective of choice to describe an unreliable goalkeeper is *dodgy*. A chorus of '**dodgy keeper**' is a popular chant when the other team's goalkeeper fumbles a cross or allows a shot to squirm under his body.

● dogfight

The fierce and desperate struggle at the bottom of the table between teams in danger of relegation is routinely described as a **dogfight**: 'Everton are in danger of being dragged into the relegation dogfight.' A dogfight is, of course, combat at close quarters between fighter aircraft, though the more likely image is the literal one of dogs actually snarling and snapping at one another.

Do I not like that

One of football's most famous managerial remarks was uttered on 13 October 1993 by the England manager Graham Taylor during England's 2–0 defeat to Holland in a World Cup qualifier in Rotterdam. Taylor responded to a controversial Ronald Koeman goal for the Dutch by muttering the curiously garbled '**Do I not like that**', an imperishable moment captured in a fly-on-the-wall (or, in this case, fly-on-the-touchline) TV documentary *An Impossible Job*. A national catchphrase was born.

dolly

In cricket, a **dolly** is a very simple catch, usually when the ball lobs gently to the fielder from the bat. The word probably derives from an Anglo-Indian word meaning an offering of fruit or flowers, presented on a tray. An easy catch is similarly 'served up on a plate' to the fielder. The word can also be used as a verb:

The Kiwis' plight worsened when McGrath coaxed Astle to dolly a catch to Justin Langer at mid-wicket. iafrica.com, 28/11/04

domestique

In the ecology of a cycling team, the **domestiques** (literally 'servants' in French) are the self-sacrificing skivvies or worker bees, whose main job is to ride for the good of the team, and in particular the team leader. Their duties include fetching and carrying food and drink from the team car, catching breakaway riders, sheltering the team leader from bad weather, even giving up their bike to a team member if necessary.

donkey

A footballer thought to lack technical skill and relying more on his physical presence on the pitch invariably attracts the fans' favourite insult of **donkey**, a particular application of the more general use of the word to mean a stupid or inept person.

● donkey drop

Donkey drop is a cricketing term for a slow ball that comes to the batsman with a high curving trajectory. Such deliveries are usually easy for the batsman to hit.

● doosra

A fairly recent addition to the cricketing lexicon, a **doosra** is a type of delivery, the off-spin bowler's equivalent of a 'googly', in that it spins in the opposite direction to the bowler's usual delivery. Developed in the late 1990s by the Pakistani finger spinner Saqlain Mushtaq, the *doosra* turns the 'wrong way', that is, spinning from the off side to the leg side to a right-handed batsman. The word comes from Hindi or Urdu and means 'second' or 'other'. *See also* GOOGLY.

● dormie

In match-play golf, a player who is **dormie** is ahead by the same number of holes as there are holes left to play, and so cannot lose the match. The worst that could happen is that the match could be tied. You usually specify the number of holes left, as in 'she made a birdie on the 15th to go dormie three'. The origin of the word *dormie* is not certain but it may derive from the Latin verb *dormire* (or French *dormir*) meaning 'to sleep'. Why? Because a player who is dormie could go to sleep and they still wouldn't lose. The term has been adopted by other sports. For example, a cricket team could be described as 'dormie one' if, say, they are one up with only the final match of a Test series to go. They can tie the series but can't lose it. Another sleep-related sporting expression is **wake-up call**.

● dot ball

In cricket, a **dot ball** is a delivery from which no runs are scored and no wicket is taken. It is so-called because to record such a ball the scorer puts a single dot in the scorebook:

Getting wickets brings pressure, but bowling dot balls and getting balls in the right areas does it as well. Michael Vaughan, 21/7/04

● double handed

A jockey who is said to be **double handed** is restraining his horse with the reins, particularly in the latter stages of a race. The idea is that as soon as he lets the reins go the horse will produce a burst of speed at the end to win.

● double top

In darts, **double top** is the double 20 segment on a dartboard, right at the top: 'He's going for double top.' *See also* TOPS.

● down to the wire

If a situation goes **down to the wire**, the outcome isn't decided until the last minute. The expression comes from horse racing and originally referred to the wire stretched across and above the finishing line on a racecourse.

● downtown

On a basketball court, to score from **downtown** is to do so from the area beyond the three-point line, far away from the basket.

● drain

A golfer **drains** a putt when he holes it, as smoothly and cleanly as water flowing down a plughole. Similarly, a basketball player can be said to **drain** a three-pointer.

● dream team

Although the phrase **dream team** dates back to the 1970s in the US, it became chiefly associated with the US men's basketball team that won the gold medal at the 1992 Barcelona Olympics. Dubbed the Dream Team, this all-star line-up comprised the cream of professional basketball talent at the time, including Larry Bird, Magic Johnson and Michael Jordan. The term can be applied more widely to any team (whether in sport or otherwise) assembled from a seemingly ideal combination of individuals. *See also* GALACTICO.

● drill

Sportswriters and commentators use the verb **drill** to describe a hard, fast, straight shot or cross, especially one that keeps fairly low:

[Lampard] broke into the box with a surging run and then drilled the ball past Butina. bbc.co.uk, 21/6/04

● drop

'Defeat leaves Palace facing the drop': a team **facing the drop** is in danger of relegation to the division below. Relegation is commonly talked about using the metaphor of a trapdoor and, in the days of public executions, the **drop** was the trapdoor on the gallows through which the person being hanged fell. *See also* DROP ZONE, TRAPDOOR

● drop zone

The **drop zone** is a variation on the idea of the exit from the bottom of the table as a trapdoor:

[Everton] remain 16th in the Premiership table but are now six points clear of the drop zone having picked up 12 points from their last five outings. iol.co.za, 3/12/05

The term **drop zone** is used to denote the area into which troops or supplies are dropped by parachute, and in parachuting and skydiving is the area where a parachutist is expected to land.

TENSES

Football commentators generally, though not exclusively, use the **❝ present tense ❞** while describing live action ('Ronaldinho slips the ball to Kaka'), or do without verbs altogether ('Cole to Rooney'). To talk about an incident that has just occurred a radio commentator is likely to use the **❝ past tense ❞** ('He went down much too easily') whereas his television counterpart, reviewing the same incident while it is being replayed on the screen for the viewers, might well use the present tense ('Look, he goes down much too easily there'). The real linguistic curiosity comes when, in a post-match interview, a player is asked to recall and talk through an incident in the match that he has recently been participating in, particularly when asked to supply the narrative to a video replay. In such circumstances a player will often adopt the **❝ present perfect tense ❞**, not quite in the present, not quite in the past ('I've got past the defender, I've knocked it on to Crouchy and the big man's stuck it in'). Another notable use of verb tense is switching into the **❝ historical present ❞**, often giving a dramatic immediacy to a recalled account of an incident: 'We had a couple of chances where if it goes in, the game's dead and buried.' *See also* POST-MATCH INTERVIEW p.50 and GRAMMAR p.80

● duck

A **duck** in cricket is a score of nought by a dismissed batsman. This usage dates from the second half of the 19th century and is a shortening of its original form **duck's egg**, because of the egg shape of the number 0. The equivalent term in baseball is **goose egg**. A batsman is 'out for a duck' or 'gets (or makes or scores) a duck'. To **break your duck** is to score the first run of your innings, but in general usage outside cricket simply means to achieve your first win or success. *See also* DIAMOND DUCK, GOLDEN DUCK, GOLDEN PAIR, KING PAIR, PAIR.

● ducks on the pond

A choice item of baseball commentator-speak, **ducks on the pond** describes the sight of runners on the bases, especially when the bases are loaded (that is, there are runners on the first, second and third bases). The expression is thought to have been coined by the broadcaster Arch McDonald.

Lewis stole second and Clint Eury walked to put a pair of ducks on the pond. monmouth.edu, 7/3/05

● Duckworth-Lewis method

The **Duckworth-Lewis method** is a somewhat baffling statistical method for calculating the revised target score required by a team batting second in a one-day cricket match that has been interrupted by rain delays. It was devised by the statistician Frank Duckworth and the mathematician Tony Lewis in the 1990s.

● dugout

The **dugout** is the low shelter at the side of a football or baseball pitch where a team's manager, coaches and substitutes sit during a game. The first dugout on a football pitch was built by the Aberdeen coach Donald Colman in the 1920s, so that he could better observe his players' footwork from the touchline. Reactions 'from the dugout' can be as entertaining as what is happening on the pitch.

Martin O'Neill's animated behaviour in the dugout surely has its roots in his restless playing days. Independent on Sunday, 8/5/05

Mourinho was banished from the dugout for two matches. theage.com.au, 7/4/05

● dunk

In basketball, a player **dunks** the ball when he jumps up and pushes it down through the hoop from above instead of throwing it in from a distance. This meaning derives from the idea of dipping a biscuit or doughnut into a drink. *See also* SLAM DUNK.

● dying quail

What is it about sport and quails, linguistically speaking? In a fine example of baseball lingo, a **dying quail** is a softly struck ball that, once it leaves the bat, loops into the air and drops suddenly and unexpectedly between the infield and the outfield, supposedly resembling the trajectory of a bird shot in flight. *See also* QUAIL HIGH.

e

eagle

If an eagle is a big bird, then an **eagle** in golf is a big 'birdie', a score of two under par on a particular hole. **Eagle** can also be used as a verb: 'Mickelson eagled the par-five 11th.' *See also* ALBATROSS, BIRDIE.

early doors

'If Arsenal get a goal early doors then it should be easy for them': the curious turn of phrase **early doors**, meaning 'in the opening minutes of the game' was famously introduced by Ron Atkinson, and is now widespread among players and commentators alike. Previously, **early doors** referred to the quiet time in a pub, shortly after opening time.

educated

Like 'cultured', the word **educated** can be applied not to a footballer's mind but to his foot, almost exclusively the left one. It suggests a high level of technical expertise. *See also* CULTURED.

embryo chaser

An **embryo chaser** is a horse who looks good enough in hurdle races to have a future over the larger fences in steeplechases.

● encroachment

In football, the term **encroachment** (one of those oddly formal words familiar to football fans, like **simulation**) is used for the offence of a player running into the penalty area before a penalty kick is taken. In American football, the term describes a similar transgression, when a player runs across the line of scrimmage and makes contact with an opposing player before the snap (that is, when the ball is put into play by being passed backwards).

● end-to-end

Football commentators will say 'it's **end-to-end** stuff' to describe an exciting, flowing game with plenty of attacking play and scoring opportunities at both ends of the pitch. *See also* BOX-TO-BOX.

● engine

A footballer or other sportsman described as having 'a good **engine**' possesses considerable energy and stamina: 'a quick midfield player with a great engine'.

● engine room

A football team's midfield can be described as the **engine room**, where the team's power and forward movement is generated. The term derives from rowing where it designates the four members of a crew of eight, normally the most powerful rowers, who sit in the middle of the boat.

● express yourself

In sport, **expressing yourself** is playing with uninhibited flair and creativity. Gifted players welcome the opportunity to do this:

As soon as I walk on to the pitch, I want to express myself, do the best I can, and forget the nerves. Wayne Rooney, 23/4/06

● eye for goal

A footballer, particularly a striker, who consistently scores goals can be said to have an **eye for goal**: 'Henry has lightning pace and a great eye for goal.' An alternative expression is 'he knows where the goal is'.

f

fancy dan

The term **fancy dan** is an uncomplimentary label for a football player, typically a foreign player, whose ostentatious skill on the ball can seem a frivolous luxury in the full-blooded English game. Managers may prefer less naturally gifted players who work hard and are prepared to 'get stuck in' rather than indulge themselves with their party pieces. *See also* SHOW PONY.

farm the strike

A skilled batsman is said to **farm the strike** (or **farm the bowling**) during the course of a cricket match when, with a less able batting partner at the other end, he deliberately contrives to face as much of the bowling as possible, for example by taking a single off the last ball of each over:

Farming the strike cleverly, Cairns hit four sixes, 10 fours and a five in little more than an hour at the wicket. dailytimes.com.pk, 22/5/04

See also AGRICULTURAL SHOT.

featherbed

In cricket parlance, a **featherbed** is a pitch that is comfortable for batting on, slow-paced and offering little help to bowlers,

such as many of the pitches in India and Pakistan. *See also* BED
AND BREAKFAST.

● ferret

In cricket, if a 'rabbit' is a poor batsman, then a **ferret** is a very
poor batsman indeed, so-called because a ferret 'goes in after the
rabbits'. *See also* RABBIT.

● fifer

A bowler's feat of taking five or more wickets in an innings of a
cricket match (comparable to a batsman scoring a century) is
known as a **fifer** or **five-for**. This comes from the wording
conventionally used to talk about a bowler's performance in a
match. If he takes five wickets and concedes, say, 120 runs, he is
said to have figures of **5 for** 120. *See also* MICHELLE.

● fifty-fifty

A **fifty-fifty** or **fifty-fifty ball** is a situation in a football match
when the ball is loose, temporarily in neither team's possession,
and two players from opposing teams are bearing down on it from
different directions and about the same distance away. Given that
each player has an equal chance of getting there first, it is often
taken as a sign of a team's commitment and competitive spirit
whether or not they tend to 'win the fifty-fifties': 'Grimsby are
keener than Fulham and are winning most of the fifty-fifties.'

● fill your boots

To **fill your boots** is to take full advantage of an opportunity,
often to help yourself to runs or goals against inferior opposition:
'Andrew Strauss filled his boots against the Bangladesh attack',
'Aussie batters fill their boots', 'Van Nistelrooy could fill his boots
against the Villa defence'.

filth

Filth is a colloquial cricketing term for extremely poor bowling, as in 'his first ball was short leg-stump filth'.

final third

The **final third** is a technical-sounding way of referring to the part of the football pitch upfield nearest to the opposition's goal, the business end, as it were, where the goals are scored:

We looked okay and had plenty of possession but I was disappointed by our attacking play in the final third. Chris Coleman, Fulham manager, 26/9/05

fishing

In cricket, **fishing** is attempting to hit the ball by holding the bat away from the body outside the off stump and either missing the ball completely or edging it behind. The batsman's action resembles an angler dangling his line in the water and there is also perhaps a suggestion of **fish** in the sense 'search or grope around for something'.

Mohammad Rafique was caught behind first ball, fishing outside off-stump. bbc.co.uk, 28/5/05

fishtail

A motor-racing car is said to **fishtail** if the rear end swings uncontrollably from side to side.

flag to flag

A racing driver wins **flag to flag** when he starts a race in **pole position** (that is, at the front of the starting grid) and wins without ever being passed by another car. Motor races are started with lights these days, but traditionally the host country's national flag was used. A black-and-white chequered flag is still waved at the finish.

Fernando Alonso led flag-to-flag today at Magny Cours to win the French GP, his 5th win of the season. autoracing1.com, 3/7/05

Flag to Flag Win for Fisichella headline, uk.sports.yahoo.com, 19/3/06

● flat back four

A football team's back four is its four-man defence, and if it's a **flat back four** they play in a line across the pitch, often moving forward as a unit to 'spring the offside trap'.

● flat-track bully

The expression **flat-track bully** refers to a batsman who is able to dominate bowling attacks and score prolifically on cricket pitches that don't offer much assistance to the bowlers but is much less successful against the best bowlers in good bowling conditions, particularly at Test level. The term was coined by the New Zealand cricketer and coach John Bracewell, describing the Zimbabwean-born England batsman Graeme Hick.

● flea flicker

A **flea flicker** is a deceptive 'play' or manoeuvre in American football in which the ball is quickly transferred between teammates sideways or backwards.

He used a flea flicker to hit Glenn on a 70-yard touchdown pass. sportingnews.com, 19/9/05

● focus

Focus is the term used by sports psychologists, and increasingly by the players themselves, for what the rest of us call concentration, in particular giving all your attention to the play and tuning out all outside distractions:

Philippoussis seems to have lost his focus during the rain-break and is immediately broken as Popp takes the set 6–4. bbc.co.uk, 2/7/03

Things went my way; I holed some long putts and some par-saving putts. I was telling myself 20 times a hole, 'keep your focus'. Michael Campbell, US Open champion, 19/7/05

See also IN THE ZONE.

● footballing

The adjective **footballing** doesn't simply mean 'playing football'. The word also suggests quality, skill and attractiveness in the football being played:

Knowing what a good footballing side Ipswich are, I expect it will be a night to enjoy from a football connoisseur's point of view. Steve Wigley, Southampton director of youth football, 18/4/05

● fore

Fore is a warning cry used by golfers as they strike the ball, to let people ahead know that they may be standing in its path. It is probably short for 'before' or 'afore'.

● for fun

Meaning 'with ease, effortlessly', **for fun** is a football commentators' expression, originally popularized by Ron Atkinson. A particular player, it might be said (and often is), 'is scoring goals for fun at the moment' or 'goes past defenders for fun'.

● form is temporary, class is permanent

Players suffering criticism during a streak of poor performances will often hit back with the now-clichéd aphorism, '**form is temporary, class is permanent**'. Ian Botham once wore a T-shirt printed with this wording. *See also* CLASS.

● fortress

When a team proves particularly difficult to beat at home, they can be said to have turned their home ground into a **fortress**: 'Newcastle United are starting to turn St James' Park into a fortress', 'Bolton travel to fortress Highbury to take on Arsenal'. In rugby, 'fortress Twickenham' became a journalistic cliché during the early 2000s when England proved unbeatable on home soil. The term is often used ironically by opposing fans whose team manages to breach the supposedly impregnable 'fortress':

United fortress turning into bouncy castle. telegraph.co.uk, 23/10/05

● fourth official

Sounding like a shadowy and rather sinister figure from the world of a Graham Greene or John Le Carré novel, the **fourth official** is a relative newcomer to the game of football. Introduced into the game in 1991, the fourth official assists the other three (the referee and two assistant referees, the officials formerly known as linesmen). His or her duties include overseeing substitutions, maintaining off-pitch discipline among the substitutes and coaching staff, and reporting any incidents the referee might have missed. Most visibly perhaps, it is the fourth official who signals the number of minutes of added time at the end of a match.

● fresh legs

A player may be replaced towards the end of a game not because he's injured or for tactical reasons but simply because the player is tired. Then it's time for **fresh legs**, belonging to the substitute. A related commentators' cliché is the observation that 'there are some tired legs out there'.

● fried egg

In golf, the term **fried-egg** lie describes the position of the ball when it is half-buried in the sand of a bunker. *See also* BIRD'S NEST.

● front nine

The **front nine** is the first half of a round of golf, consisting of the first nine holes numbered 1 to 9: 'he struggled on the front nine', 'she played the front nine in one under'. *See also* BACK NINE.

● front up

In sporting usage, **front up** means 'perform well when necessary' or 'deliver the goods', with an additional suggestion of a bruising, chest-to-chest encounter. As with a number of other examples of sportspeak, it comes from Australia, a refinement of its basic meaning 'make an appearance, turn up':

If your forwards don't front up in winter you can forget about being a force in the Premiership. Brian Smith, London Irish coach, 27/12/05

Hussain, Thorpe, Trescothick and Butcher fronted up for England in Wellington, while New Zealand's top order has not yet delivered when runs have really been needed. bbc.co.uk, 29/3/02

● frozen rope

In baseball, a ball hit very hard that flies low and in a straight line is sometimes described, rather vividly, as a **frozen rope** (or simply as a **rope**), as in 'he hit a frozen rope to left centrefield'.

g

gaffer

The **gaffer** (probably deriving originally from the word *godfather*) is, colloquially, the boss, the manager of a football team. Rafael Benitez, the Liverpool manager since 2004, is known as 'Rafa the gaffer'.

galacticos

Los Galacticos (literally, 'the galactics') is the nickname, coined by the Spanish sports daily *Marca*, for the group of star players signed by the Spanish football club Real Madrid during Florentino Pérez's tenure as club president (2000–6). A high-profile player was signed in consecutive summers: Luis Figo in 2000, Zinedine Zidane in 2001, Ronaldo in 2002 and David Beckham in 2003. These players, together with the homegrown Spanish player Raul, were collectively referred to as the galacticos. *See also* DREAM TEAM.

game needs a goal

Faced with a 0–0 scoreline and a match that has lacked any excitement, football commentators frequently resort to the clichéd observation **the game needs a goal**.

game on

The exclamation **game on** announces, often during a commentary or an account of a match, that anyone can still win and the real action is still to come. It is typically used when the player or team who appeared no longer to have a chance of winning has just got themselves back into the contest. The expression comes from the game of darts, where it is a call for silence, signalling the start of play.

All of a sudden we've got a wee bit jangly nerves, they've got another goal back and it's game on. John Gorman, Wycombe Wanderers manager, 30/4/05

Just when England look home and hosed, Collingwood dabs one to Ponting, who takes a desperate catch at silly point. Game on! Sean Ingle, Guardian Unlimited, 12/9/05

game plan

The term **game plan** was originally used only in American football, denoting a pre-arranged strategy meticulously worked out by the coach and players for winning a particular game. In general usage, in both American and British English, the term has come to refer to any step-by-step strategy for achieving something carefully worked out in advance.

gardening

Sometimes a batsman can be seen stepping away from his crease between deliveries and prodding lightly at the pitch with the end of his bat, apparently flattening out any rough patches or divots in the surface of the pitch. Often this activity, known as **gardening**, is to give the batsman an opportunity to calm his nerves after a particularly good delivery before facing the next ball.

g.r.a.m.m.a.r

Players and managers have traditionally been mocked for their syntax when commenting that 'the lads played tremendous' or 'the goalie done brilliant'. However, sports language should generally be celebrated for its inventive way with parts of speech.

Nouns are routinely used as verbs. For example, a tennis player **aces** his opponent, a golfer **birdies** a hole or **cards** a good score, an American football player **clotheslines** another player or is **benched**, a batsman **middles** the ball or is **gated** by the bowler, a racing driver **pits** during a race, an athlete **medals** at a championships.

Conversely, verbs can be made into nouns, as with a **get** in tennis, a **give-and-go** in football, a **steal** in basketball, an **assist** in various sports. An adjective can become a noun (a **quick**, in cricket) or an adverb (win **ugly**). And US sports usage has produced a choice pair of grammar-defying superlative adjectives in **losingest** and **winningest**. *See also* TENSES p.65

garryowen

Also known as an 'up-and-under', a **garryowen** is a very high kick that keeps the ball in the air long enough for the kicker and his teammates to rush forward to catch it and which is intended to put pressure on the defending player trying to catch the ball. The word comes from Garryowen rugby club in Limerick, Ireland, where the tactic was much used. *See also* UP-AND-UNDER.

gas

Gas is baseball slang for a pitch thrown at maximum speed, as in 'throw gas', 'pump gas' or 'give him the gas'. The idea is of someone accelerating in a car by putting his foot down on the gas pedal. A pitcher can also be said to 'gas it up'. *See also* HEAT, NOTHING LEFT IN THE TANK.

gate

If a batsman is bowled **through the gate**, the ball hits his wicket after first passing through the gap he leaves between his bat and his pad as he plays a stroke. **Gate** can also be used as a verb, as in 'Trescothick was gated by a superb Collymore inswinger'.

get

In tennis, a **get** is a return that a player successfully makes, although it looked as though he or she wouldn't be able to reach it. It tends to be used in conjunction with words like 'good' and 'great': 'What a great get by his opponent.'

get big on

A ball **gets big on** a batsman when it reaches him more quickly and perhaps further up the pitch than he expected it to:

The breakthrough he deserved came his way after the delay, Ponting edging a ball that got big on him to Strauss at gully. bbc.co.uk, 10/9/05

● get down

In golf, to **get down** in a particular number of strokes is to take that many strokes to put the ball into the hole, either from the tee or from a spot where the ball has landed: 'she got down in three for another birdie', 'he'll struggle to get down in two from there'.

● get legs

Golfers shout **get legs** (or **get up**) after hitting a shot in order to encourage the ball to roll a bit further when they think it may stop too short. This is a case of a golfer literally **addressing** the ball.

● get the trip

The 'trip' in horse racing is the race distance. A horse that **gets the trip** is one that is able to stay the distance of the race:

Virginia Waters, the other joint-favourite, weaved her way through the pack after the turn for hom but did not get the trip, finishing fourth. bbc.co.uk, 3/6/05

It was clear before yesterday's race that Kicking King was the class horse left in it, and that he'd win if he got the trip, which he clearly did. guardian.co.uk, 19/3/05

See also TRIP.

● get to first base

The phrase **get to** (or **make**) **first base**, meaning 'reach the first stage of a process', derives from baseball. First base is where a batter must run to after hitting the ball, the first step towards scoring a run. *See also* COVER ALL THE BASES, OFF BASE, TOUCH BASE.

● gimme

Gimme or **gimmie** (a contraction of 'give it to me') is a golfing term for a putt that is so short that, sportingly, your opponent is happy to concede it. He doesn't think you would miss it and so you are allowed to pick the ball up without actually having to make the putt. In wider use, a **gimme** is something that is very easy to do or achieve, or a foregone conclusion. An easy question in a quiz could be described as a gimme, or someone might say, 'Actually I don't think it's a gimme that they're going to win.'

● give and go

A **give and go** (also known as a **one-two** or **wall pass**) in football is when one player passes to a teammate and runs on past an opponent to receive an immediate return pass. The term is also used in hockey and basketball.

● glass jaw

A boxer who is described as having a **glass jaw** (or a **glass chin**) is susceptible to being knocked out, or at least hurt, by hard punches to the head. *See also* CHIN.

● goal drought

A period of time during which a football player (especially a striker) or team has failed to score is often described as a **goal drought**. The duration of this lean spell is sometimes specified, as in 'a ten-game goal drought' or 'a four-month goal drought'. The player seeks to 'end' or 'break' the goal drought:

The lead was doubled early in the second half as Paul Scholes ended his seven month goal drought with a superb far post volley from a Darren Fletcher cross. soccer-europe.com, 21/11/04

And although Rafael Benitez continues to play down the forward's goal drought, Crouch's body language plainly reveals just how desperate he is to get off the mark. Guardian, 7/11/05

● goal machine

A prolific goalscorer is sometimes dubbed a **goal machine**. The term can be used ironically when a player not known for scoring goals unexpectedly finds the back of the net a couple of times.

● goat

In American team sports like baseball and American football, a player can find himself about to be cast either as hero or **goat**. A hero-or-goat situation is a highly pressurized one in the final moments of a game when a player either has the opportunity of winning the game for his team or of being responsible for the team losing. Goat is short for 'scapegoat':

When you pitch in the eighth or ninth inning, you're either a hero or goat. There's no real in between. Phil Garner, Detroit Tigers manager, 27/5/2000

● going

In horse racing, the **going** is the official description of the state of the racing surface at a particular racecourse in terms of the amount of moisture in the ground, hence terms such as 'heavy', 'soft', 'firm' and so on.

● go in the tank

To **go in the tank** is to deliberately lose a boxing match, especially in return for a bribe. 'Tank' here means swimming pool, so the expression is really a variation of the more familiar phrase 'take a dive'. *See also* TANK.

● golden arm

Sometimes a cricketer who bowls only infrequently, usually referred to as an 'occasional bowler', has the knack of getting a wicket when the regular specialist bowlers don't seem able to make a breakthrough. Such a player is said to have a **golden arm**:

Tendulkar turned his golden arm for a tantalising haul of three wickets for 10 runs. tribuneindia.com, 26/2/2000

● golden duck

If a **duck** – getting out in cricket for a score of nought – is bad, a **golden duck** is even worse. This is getting out for nought off the first ball you face in your (very short) innings.

● golden pair

Two **golden ducks** make a **golden pair** (also known as a **king pair**). In other words, a batsman suffers the ignominy of a golden pair if he is dismissed for a score of nought off the first ball he faces in each of his innings in a two-innings match.

● golden sombrero

If a batter's striking out three times in a baseball game can be described as a **hat trick**, then the even greater ignominy of striking out four times earns the unwanted tag **golden sombrero**. Bigger failure, bigger hat.

Armando Rios, struggling at the plate lately, hit a ground out to second in the bottom of the eighth to avoid the 'golden sombrero' of four consecutive strikeouts. nysportsday.com, 22/9/05

● go looking for work

In rugby, a winger who doesn't feel he's seeing enough of the ball during a match might decide to move infield for a period in an effort to get more involved in the game. A player who does this **goes looking for work**:

He is a creator, he goes looking for work and he pops up in unusual places which makes him difficult for defences to handle. Graham Henry, Lions coach, on Jason Robinson, 2/6/01

See also BAD DAY AT THE OFFICE.

● good

A tennis umpire, who says during the course of a match that a particular shot by a player was **good**, isn't offering a compliment. He or she is saying that the ball landed in the court.

● google

The most common use of the verb **google** nowadays is without doubt in the context of using the Google internet search engine. In cricket, though, a spin bowler who bowls a **googly** can be said to **google** the ball. Curiously, the name of another search engine, Yahoo, is also a piece of cricketing jargon. *See also* YAHOO.

● googly

Even people completely uninterested in cricket have heard of a **googly**, probably because it's such an odd-sounding word. In technical terms, a googly is a deceptive delivery bowled by a leg spin bowler that moves after pitching from the off side to the leg side (unlike a normal leg break), when bowling to a right-handed batsman. In less technical terms, it spins the opposite way (that is, from left to right) to the way the batsman is expecting it to spin. The origin of the term isn't certain, although the most likely explanation is that when the English cricketer B. J. T. Bosanquet developed this type of delivery in the early 1900s, batsmen were so bamboozled that they goggled (or 'googled', a variant form of the word) in surprise. *See also* BOSIE, WRONG'UN.

● goose egg

In American sport, especially baseball, a **goose egg** is a score of zero, from the egg shape of the number. For added effect, it can be described as 'a big fat goose egg'. The usage, which parallels the cricketing term 'duck' (originally 'duck's egg'), dates back to the 1880s.

It was the first time since April 3 of last year that the Red Hawks put a goose egg on the board. poly.rpi.edu, 20/4/05

See also DUCK.

go the distance

In boxing, a bout (or a boxer) **goes the distance** when it (or he) lasts the full number of scheduled rounds. In baseball, the expression is used to describe a pitcher pitching an entire game. The use of 'distance' in both cases is slightly curious, as it refers to a length of time rather than the length of the space between two points. In general usage, to **go the distance** is to complete a course of action.

go to school

By first taking careful note of a playing partner's putt that is on a similar line to his, a golfer can learn the line and pace he needs when making his own putt. This is known as **going to school**:

Mickelson was able to watch Di Marco's putt (it missed) and go to school on his line, a nasty right-to-lefter. theage.com.au, 13/4/04

Woods had almost the exact same birdie putt and went to school on Monty's putt, lagging it to tap-in range. golfonline.com, 17/7/05

go yard

To **go yard** is to hit a home run in baseball. It is probably an elliptical version of 'hit the ball out of the yard', where 'yard' is a colloquial term for a ballpark and its perimeter.

grand salami

In baseball, a grand slam is the hitting of a home run with runners on all three bases, scoring four runs. Informally this is known as a **grand salami**.

green in regulation

Good golfers are expected to reach (or hit) the **green in regulation**, that is, to reach the putting surface from the tee in two strokes fewer than par, the assumption being that two putts will generally be needed on the green to get the ball in the hole.

● green top

A cricket pitch with plenty of green grass still visible, a sign of moisture in the pitch, is known as a **green top**. Fast bowlers smack their lips in anticipation before bowling on such pitches, as the ball is likely to bounce off the pitch quickly and unpredictably for the batsman.

● gridiron

An American football playing field, marked out in a grid of lines that cross the field at 5-yard intervals, is often called the **gridiron**, because it resembles a grill used to cook meat on. The word can also be used to refer to the sport itself, as in 'to watch gridiron', though this use is more common outside the US.

● Group of Death

In the early group stages of every football tournament, particularly the World Cup, there always seems to be a so-called **Group of Death**, a tough group of well-matched teams, the outcome of which is difficult to predict. The phrase has become a cliché, but it is almost obligatory now for one of the groups to be dubbed the Group of Death by the press. In the 2002 World Cup, this was generally considered to be Group F, made up of England, Argentina, Nigeria and Sweden.

● grubber

A **grubber** (or **grubber kick**) is a kick in rugby that sends the ball bouncing and rolling forwards along the ground. In cricket, the term is used for a ball that keeps very low after bouncing off the pitch, making it difficult for the batsman to play it. *See also* SHOOTER.

● gruppetto

Italian for 'small group', the **gruppetto** is the group of riders, the slow climbers, at the back of the field on mountain stages in cycling races such as the Tour de France. They stick together to help each other complete the stage within the time limit. *See also* AUTOBUS.

gully

In cricket parlance, **gully** is a close fielding position on the off side and just behind the line of the batsman's wicket. This position is called the gully because it occupies the gap or channel between two other fielding positions, the slips and point.

gunner

A **gunner** in basketball is a player who takes every possible opportunity to take a long-range shot rather than, say, passing to a teammate in a more favourable position. *See also* RUN AND GUN.

h

Hail Mary

It is sometimes said of a team facing superior opponents that they haven't got a prayer. Well they have in American football, the Hail Mary. Named after the prayer to the Virgin Mary used by Roman Catholics, a **Hail Mary** (or **Hail Mary pass**) is a long high pass thrown in desperation into the end zone (the area behind the goal line) by the quarterback in the final seconds of a half or a game. The pass is not targeted at any teammate in particular and consequently appears to require divine intervention to be caught. The term was popularized by the Dallas Cowboys quarterback Roger Staubach in 1975 when he described such a last-ditch pass to receiver Drew Pearson, made to win the NFC semifinal playoff, as 'just a Hail Mary pass, a very, very lucky play'.

ham and egger

Ham and egger is a disparaging term for a boxer of mediocre ability, not likely ever to win major titles or prize money but only enough to pay for a ham-and-egg meal. Rocky Balboa, at the start of the 1976 film *Rocky*, is the archetypal ham and egger. *See also* PALOOKA, TOMATO CAN.

ham-and-egging

In match-play golf, players who perform effectively as a team by playing well at different times, say on alternate holes, are said to be **ham-and-egging**. In American English the term can be used more widely when describing two people with complementary skills.

The whiz kid from Spain had been sensational in teaming with Parnevik for four matches, but lost amid their spectacular recovery shots and seamless ham-and-egging was the fact that Garcia was not striking the ball well. sportsillustrated.cnn.com, 4/10/99

See also FRIED EGG.

hammer

A cyclist who is riding hard in a race, going all out, is said to be **hammering** or **putting the hammer down**: 'Armstrong puts the hammer down and takes back the yellow jersey.' A variation is 'throw down the hammer'.

handbags

A scuffle or verbal spat between two or more players in which there is a fair bit of pushing and shoving but no actual throwing of punches is often described by commentators as a case of **handbags**, or in the longer form **handbags at ten paces**:

I have watched the video and Dichio hardly made contact, it was handbags at ten paces. Billy Davies, Preston North End manager, 24/9/05

A duel with handbags rather than pistols is clearly not to be taken too seriously and is not really a proper fight at all but a somewhat effeminate version of one. The term may partly be influenced by the image of Margaret Thatcher using her handbag as a weapon during her premiership, when she was said to **handbag** political opponents, including members of her own Cabinet.

RHYMING

Many sporting expressions are memorable and pleasing to the ear because they have a rhyming or alliterative form. American sport is particularly fond of such **RHYMING** expressions as **run and gun**, **shake and bake** and **shine the pine**. Interestingly, none of these expressions work so well in the past tense. Other examples of rhyming phrases include **crash of ash**, **sin bin**, **rope-a-dope** and **splash and dash**. A couple of pieces of cricket jargon employ the rhyming slang technique of dropping the second element that actually supplies the rhyme, hence **bunsen** (burner/turner – a good pitch for spinning) and **Michelle** (Pfeiffer/fifer – a bowler's haul of five wickets). Nicknames for sporting contests, especially boxing matches, often catch on because they follow the rhyming template of the **Rumble in the Jungle** (which, of course, doesn't quite rhyme at all), **Thrilla in Manila** and **War on the Shore**. **ALLITERATION** is also a common device. Among a host of examples are **big boys**, **buffet bowling**, **call a cab**, **can of corn**, **catch a crab**, **chip and charge**, **coffin corner**, **cow corner**, **crowd catch**, **dig deep**, **flea flicker**, **give-and-go**, **hold-up horse**, **nervous nineties**, **truck and trailer** and **up-and-under**.

● handicap snip

If a racehorse is described as 'something of a **handicap snip**', the weight it has been allotted by the official handicapper for a particular race, in line with its ability and past performances, is considered to be too low, and therefore the horse is expected to have a good chance of winning. *See also* BLOT ON THE HANDICAP.

● Hand of God

The phrase **Hand of God** (*Mano de Dios* in Spanish) refers to Diego Maradona's notorious goal for Argentina against England in a quarter-final of the 1986 World Cup. Challenging for a ball with the England goalkeeper Peter Shilton, Maradona punched the ball into the net with his left fist. The infringement wasn't spotted by the referee or the linesman and the goal was allowed to stand. To add insult to injury, Maradona claimed in a post-match interview that the goal was scored 'a little bit by the Hand of God, another bit by the head of Maradona'. Another example of supposedly divine intervention in sport is American football's 'Immaculate Reception'. *See also* HAIL MARY, IMMACULATE RECEPTION.

● hands and heels

Riding a horse without having to resort to the whip is known as riding **hands and heels**:

The easy to back favourite went on at the second last and only had to be ridden out hands and heels after the last to beat Creme D'arblay by two lengths. irish-racing.com, 5/3/06

● hang time

In basketball, **hang time** is the length of time that a player is able to stay in the air as he jumps for the ball or attempts a shot on the basket. It's the same idea as footballers talking about 'hanging in the air' as they leap to head the ball. In American football, the term **hang time** is also used for the length of time between a ball being kicked and it being caught or landing on the ground.

● hard yards

In rugby, the **hard yards** are the gains in territory that are the most difficult to achieve, with the forwards advancing the ball a small distance against fierce resistance from the opposing team:

We've got some good runners and steppers and some guys with serious pace, but what we want is somebody that can flatten people and make the hard yards when he has the ball. John Wells, Leicester Tigers coach, 13/7/04

More generally, the **hard yards** represent the hard work and intense effort needed to achieve success. For example, fast bowlers giving their all in their team's cause, particularly in unfavourable conditions, can be said to be 'doing the hard yards':

Flintoff and Hoggard do not surprise me any more, because they do the hard yards for me and their country all the time. Nasser Hussain, 17/6/02

● hat

After their team has drawn a tie in a round of a knockout competition and earned a replay, football managers will invariably profess themselves 'delighted to be still **in the hat**', that is, in the draw for the next round. This hat is an imaginary one, fancifully supposed to hold the numbered balls pulled out when the draw is made. In fact, a velvet bag or a glass bowl tends to be used.

● hat trick

The expression **hat trick** was first recorded in print in the 1870s to describe the feat of a bowler taking three wickets with three consecutive balls in a game of cricket. It appears that it was customary in the 19th century for this achievement to be marked by the presentation of a new hat to the player by his club. A bowler who has taken two wickets in two balls is said to be 'on a hat trick'. The expression has come to refer to any sporting feat achieved three times in quick succession, such as a football or hockey player scoring three goals in a match or a rugby player scoring three tries. 'Hat-trick hero' has become a familiar newspaper cliché. At ice hockey games fans throw hats onto the ice when a player scores a hat trick. In baseball, a batter's striking out three times in a game can be described as a hat trick. The term can also be used to describe a single, double, triple and home run hit by the same player in a game. In contexts outside sport, three successes of any kind can be described as a hat trick.

● have the ball at your feet

Considering football's enormous popularity and cultural influence, it is perhaps surprising how few everyday idioms are based on footballing metaphors, compared to those drawn from, say, baseball or boxing. A slightly old-fashioned expression that does derive from football is **have the ball at your feet**, meaning 'have the chance, or be in a good position, to do something'.

● have the wood on

To **have the wood on** someone is an Australian expression meaning to have the upper hand over them, and is often used by sportsmen when talking about a psychological advantage one player or team seems to enjoy over another:

They've had the wood on us for so long. That adds to the elation.
Stephen Fleming, New Zealand cricket captain, after his team's first Test series win over South Africa, 29/2/04

● head

In horse racing, a **head** refers to the length of a horse's head, used when describing a short winning margin. *See also* CANVAS, NOSE, SHORT HEAD.

● head tennis

The term **head tennis** describes a dull period of a football match during which the ball is simply headed back and forth between the two teams, especially from one side of the halfway line to the other: 'the first half turned into a game of head tennis', 'we were subjected to prolonged bouts of head tennis in midfield'.

● heat

Like 'gas', **heat** is pitching in baseball at high speed, as in 'the new kid really threw some heat' and 'when he gets the arm warmed up he can still bring the heat'. *See also* GAS.

● high cheese

In baseball slang, **high cheese** is a pitcher's fastball thrown high in the strike zone, around the height of the batter's head: 'Hitters can't touch his high cheese.'

● hit the wall

Marathon runners often talk about **hitting the wall**. The wall in question is metaphorical but the physical suffering it represents is real enough. The phrase describes the sudden loss of energy an athlete experiences in the closing stages of a long race, when his or her body runs out of its reserves of glycogen (stored sugar) and begins burning body fat as a fuel source instead. *See also* BONK.

● hold-up horse

In horse racing, a **hold-up horse** is one that likes to come from behind, in contrast to a front runner:

Favourite Tagula Blue made his customary slow start, but he is a confirmed hold-up horse and should have been suited by the way the race was run. racingpost.co.uk, 19/5/06

● hole in your glove

A baseball catcher or fielder who is prone to drop catches – a serial butterfingers – can be said to have a **hole in his glove**:

Mueller has also developed a rather large hole in his glove this post season. thejohnsonian.com, 28/9/04

● hole out

While holing out in golf is good, in cricket it's not so good. A golfer who **holes out** strikes the ball into the hole to complete play on that hole: 'Woods holed out from the bunker.' A batsman who **holes out**, on the other hand, is dismissed by being caught, especially near the boundary: 'Ponting holed out to Vaas at long-off.'

● homer

A **homer** is a referee who appears to favour the home team, perhaps influenced or intimidated by home support. In baseball, a **homer** is a colloquial term for a home run.

● home stretch

To be on the **home stretch** (or **home straight**) is to be in the final stage of something. This is a horse-racing metaphor: the home stretch is the last section of a racecourse just before the finish.

● honest pro

Honest pro is a slightly patronizing term for a professional footballer who is hard working and big-hearted and makes the most of his limited ability.

● hoops

The sport of basketball is colloquially known as **hoops**, referring to the metal rims around the top of each of the baskets, from which the net is suspended. Other examples of a piece of sports equipment lending its name to the sport itself include all the '-ball' sports, such as football, baseball, netball and, of course, basketball. *See also* ARROWS.

● hops

It's common to say of a basketball player with the ability to jump high off the ground that 'he's got great **hops**' or simply 'he's got hops'.

● hospital pass

A wonderfully descriptive term used in rugby and other sports, a **hospital pass** is a poorly timed (and certainly unwelcome) pass to a teammate, which puts him in immediate and unavoidable danger of receiving a crunching tackle the instant he catches the ball. In general usage the term is used to mean a job or responsibility handed to someone that seems likely to be highly problematic, a 'poisoned chalice': 'The new chairman may feel he has been thrown a hospital pass.'

● hot corner

The fielding position at third base on a baseball field is sometimes called **hot corner**. This is because it tends to be the scene of most intense activity, with batted balls coming to the fielder at great speed, giving him very little time to react. The term dates back to the early 20th century. *See also* COFFIN CORNER, COW CORNER.

● howzat

Although in practice it can sometimes resemble an inarticulate bellow, the cry of the fielding side in appealing to the umpire to give a batsman out is usually expressed as **howzat**, an abbreviation of the question asked of the umpire, 'how is that?'. Alternative forms of the appeal are 'how's that?' and 'how is he?'.

● hutch

Since batsmen can be described both as 'rabbits' and as 'bunnies',
it is perhaps not surprising that the pavilion is known informally
by cricketers as the **hutch**, especially in the context of a batsman
returning there after being dismissed: 'Both South African openers
were soon back in the hutch.' *See also* BUNNY, RABBIT.

i

Immaculate Reception

To American football fans the term **Immaculate Reception** inevitably calls to mind a game played between Pittsburgh Steelers and Oakland Raiders on 23 December 1972, in which the Steelers' running back Franco Harris received the ball in controversial circumstances to score a winning touchdown. The phrase (punning, of course, on 'Immaculate Conception') was first used on air by the US broadcaster Myron Cope. *See also* HAIL MARY.

innings

Among the more obvious linguistic differences between cricket and baseball is the use of the word **innings**. In cricket this is both the singular and plural form and denotes a team's or batsman's turn at batting. In baseball an **inning** (singular, with **innings** the plural) is each of the playing periods in a game during which both teams have a turn at batting. The word *inning* originally meant 'an act of going in', and was formed on the same lines as words like 'outing' and 'offing'.

insert

It's an oddly formal-sounding term, but if the captain of a cricket team **inserts** the other team, he puts them in to bat first after winning the toss: 'Carl Hooper won the toss and inserted India', 'England slipped to 57–3 on a drying wicket after being inserted by New Zealand'.

● interstate

All US interstate highways have two-digit numbers, hence the imaginative baseball expression 'on the **interstate**', meaning having a batting average below .100.

● in the clubhouse

Golf commentators and journalists talk about a player being 'in the clubhouse with a two-stroke lead' or 'the leader in the clubhouse at two under'. A golfer who is **in the clubhouse** has completed his round for the day, in contrast to others who are still out on the course and have not yet completed their rounds. Similarly, in cricket, a batsman who has completed his innings may be said to be 'back in the pavilion'.

● in the hole

In football, an attacking midfielder or striker who plays **in the hole** is playing in a position in front of the midfield and slightly behind the main striker (or pair of strikers):

Francesco Totti should play in the hole behind strikers Alberto Gilardino and Christian Vieri. worldcupweb.com, 2/9/05

One possible attacking formation is to play 'one up front and one in the hole'. In baseball, the phrase has two distinct meanings. A batter who is **in the hole** (or, alternatively, **in the hold**) is next but one in the batting order, waiting in the dugout below ground level. A ball that lands **in the hole** lands in the gap between two fielders, in particular between first and second basemen, or between the shortstop and the third baseman. *See also* ON DECK.

● in the jaws

'He left an eight-foot birdie putt in the jaws of the 16th hole': in golf, a putt that stops just short of the hole can be said to be **in the jaws**. In other words, it has not quite been swallowed.

● in the leather

When a putt is so close to the hole that the ball lies within the length of the leather on the putter grip, it will often be conceded in a friendly golf match without the player actually having to make the putt. Such a putt is said to be **in** (or **inside**) **the leather**.

● in the paint

To be **in the paint** on a basketball court is to be in the area of the floor around the basket, specifically the foul lane area (or key area), which is usually painted a different colour from the rest of the court: 'The Maroons opened the game with a 10–0 run, scoring eight points in the paint.' *See also* PAINT THE BLACK.

● in the plate

In horse racing, a jockey who is **in the plate** is in the saddle. This is slightly confusing, as the word **plate** is also used to refer to the lightweight horseshoe that is fitted to a racehorse's foot. A horse that **spreads a plate** loses a shoe.

Restrained in mid-division by Ruby Walsh, Strong Flow clattered the ninth and Walsh did well to stay in the plate. scotsman.com, 30/11/03

Champion Frankie Dettori, who has won on Morse in the past and knows him well, is back in the plate at Ripon today, and they once again have the look of a winning partnership. scotsman.com, 24/5/05

● in the right ballpark

If an estimate or figure is **in the right ballpark** (or, simply, **in the ballpark**), it is reasonably within the range that is likely to be correct. As with the expression 'ballpark figure', this comes from the idea that a ballpark – a baseball ground – is a large space rather than a precisely defined spot. *See also* BALLPARK FIGURE.

● in the zone

Sportspeople often talk about being **in the zone**, getting in the zone or playing in the zone. Mystical and Zen-like as this sounds, they are talking about a state of mind in which a competitor is totally absorbed in the moment and is able to achieve his or her peak level of performance, with everything in his or her game clicking into place. Characteristics of 'the zone' include intense concentration, total confidence in one's ability, loss of self-consciousness and being oblivious to what is happening around you.

Even now I still get nervous two or three days before a big run. Only these days the closer I get to the start, the more I have learnt to relax and focus. By the time I'm running, I'm completely in the zone. Paula Radcliffe, Observer, 9/5/04

Maria was on a real high, really in the zone, for the whole match. Virginia Wade on Maria Sharapova, bbc.co.uk, 3/7/04

See also COMFORT ZONE, DROP ZONE, FOCUS.

● into the channels

Like 'the hole', the **channels** are a tactically significant but imprecisely located piece of football-pitch geography. They are the narrow areas on either side of the penalty area: midfielders 'play balls **into the channels**' and forwards 'make runs into the channels'.

● in your corner

A boxer's corner is the corner of the boxing ring where he sits in the rests between rounds, and where he receives assistance and instructions from his trainer and seconds. This is the basis of the expression 'to be **in your corner**', meaning 'to be on your side, supporting and encouraging you'. *See also* COFFIN CORNER, COW CORNER.

j

jaffa

In cricketing slang, a **jaffa** is a delivery that is so well bowled that it is virtually unplayable. The term comes from the Jaffa orange, presumably because such a delivery is sweet and (from the bowler's point of view, not the batsman's) **juicy**.

jaws

On a snooker table, the **jaws** of the pocket are the curved parts of the cushion that form the pocket opening.

juicy

The word **juicy** is used in cricket to describe a poor delivery that is easy for the batsman to hit, such as 'a juicy half volley' or a 'juicy full toss'. Curiously, a 'jaffa' is an extremely good ball and so not at all juicy from the batsman's point of view. *See also* JAFFA.

jump the gun

To **jump the gun** is to act or start before the proper time, often because you want to gain an unfair advantage. The expression alludes to a runner in a race setting off before the starting gun is fired. *See also* B OF THE BANG.

k

keep your eye on the ball

In general usage, to **keep your eye on the ball** is to stay alert
and keep your attention focused on what is most important. The
metaphor comes from ball games such as football, baseball,
cricket and tennis.

keep your shape

A football team's **shape** is the particular tactical formation in
which the manager has chosen to deploy the players on the pitch.
Well-organized teams **keep their shape**. Disorganized ones lose
theirs.

keirin

A curious word (Japanese in origin and pronounced 'kay-rin') that
mystifies all but cycling fans when it crops up every four years at
the Olympic Games, the **keirin** is a track race in which cyclists
jostle for position behind a pace-setting motorcycle for a number
of laps. Just before the last lap the motorcycle peels away and the
cyclists are left to sprint for the line.

● key

On a basketball court, the **key** is the (formerly keyhole-shaped) area of the floor around each of the baskets, consisting of the foul circle, the foul lane and the free-throw line.

● kick

In athletics, a runner who has a **kick** is able to put on a burst of speed in the final stretch of a long-distance race. You can also talk about an athlete '**kicking** for the line'. A **kick** in snooker, though, is a very different proposition. This is the term for an unexpectedly bad contact between the cue ball and the ball it strikes, probably caused by a speck of chalk or dust on one of the balls, or by static electricity.

● kick into touch

In British English, if you **kick** something **into touch**, you reject it or remove it from consideration. The expression comes from rugby: a ball kicked into touch (that is, over the touchline at the side of the field) is no longer in play.

● kill

Killing a ball in tennis is striking it downwards so hard that it is impossible for the opposing player to return. A similar usage in football is to say that a player 'buries' the ball in the back of the net.

● killer ball

The **killer ball** or **pass** is the decisive one that opens up the other team's defence and presents a goalscoring opportunity. It is often mentioned because it is missing: a team is 'unable to find the killer ball' or 'lacks that final killer ball', a player 'fails to deliver the killer pass'.

King of the Mountains

The **King of the Mountains** (or **KOM**) is the title bestowed on the leading climber in the Tour de France and other cycling races. He gets to wear a red-and-white polka-dot jersey.

king pair

Whether it's called a **king pair** or a 'golden pair', it's the same thing: a batsman's being out first ball for nought in both innings of a cricket match. *See also* GOLDEN PAIR, PAIR.

kiss

In the language of snooker, a **kiss** occurs when one ball lightly touches another, as in 'a kiss on the blue'.

kiss the canvas

When a boxer is knocked to the floor, lying face down, he is said to be **kissing the canvas**: 'Judah stumbled forward and kissed the canvas a second time.'

knock

A batsman's innings can be referred to as a **knock**, particularly when expressing admiration for an entertaining, free-scoring innings. The word tends to attract adjectives like 'good', 'useful', 'gritty' and 'match-winning'. The phrase **captain's knock** is also common, as in 'Carl Hooper played a captain's knock of 112 not out'.

I

● lanterne rouge

The rider in last place in the standings in a cycling stage race is known as the **lanterne rouge** (literally 'red light' in French). The term comes from the red light at the rear of a train. *See also* WAGGING THE TAIL.

● last man

In football, the **last man** is the only defending player (other than the goalkeeper) between an opposing player and the goal who denies that player a clear goalscoring opportunity, an offence punishable by a sending off:

Steven Pressley felled Darren Young just outside the box and was deemed the last man by referee Calum Murray, who showed the red card. Scotland on Sunday, 23/10/05

● lateral

In American football, a **lateral** is a pass thrown to a teammate sideways or backwards. The word can also be used as a verb:

Linebacker Donnie Edwards intercepted a pass and lateraled to Hart, who raced 40 yards into the end zone to complete the scoring with 34 seconds left. tsn.ca, 2/2/06

● laughing group

Also known as the 'autobus' and the 'gruppetto', the **laughing group** is the group of cyclists at the back of the field on mountain stages in cycling races such as the Tour de France. They are happy to cooperate in helping one another complete the stage inside the time limit. *See also* AUTOBUS, GRUPPETTO.

● lead the line

One of the many militaristic terms from football, to **lead the line** is to be a team's main striker or pair of strikers. There is a certain nobility, even heroism, in the expression:

After the interval Cole continued to lead the line with aplomb.
fulhamfc.com, 21/8/04

● length

In horse racing it's the length of a horse and in rowing it's the length of a boat, but in both cases a **length** is a measurement of the distance between competitors in a race, as in 'Barbaro takes the Kentucky Derby by six lengths' or 'the French crew led by 1½ lengths'. *See also* CANVAS, HEAD, NOSE.

● let

In tennis, a **let** is a point that isn't allowed to stand but has to be replayed, usually because a serve just clips the top of the net before landing in the court. What's interesting about this use of *let* is that it appears to mean precisely the opposite of the most familiar meaning of the word (that is, 'to allow'). This is because it is, in fact, an extension of an entirely different word *let* meaning 'impediment or obstruction' (as in the formal phrase 'without let or hindrance') and deriving from an Old English word meaning 'to hinder'.

● Let's be 'aving you

The scene was Norwich City's ground Carrow Road on the evening
of 28 February 2005. Having seen her team throw away a 2–0 lead
against Manchester City to go in at half-time at 2–2, Norwich
director (and best-selling cookery writer) Delia Smith unexpectedly
took up the microphone to deliver the following fervent rallying
cry to the fans: 'This is a message for possibly the best supporters
in the world. We need a twelfth man here. Where are you? Where
are you? **Let's be having you**! Come on!' Her appeal failed to
inspire her team to a win, who eventually lost the game 3–2, but
'let's be 'aving you' became a comic catchphrase.

● level playing field

A **level playing field** is a situation in which everyone is
competing on equal terms. This useful metaphor comes from the
idea that a playing field that is not level may give an unfair
advantage to the home side. Before Yeovil Town football club
moved to a new ground in 1990, they famously played on just
such a sloping pitch.

● libero

In football, a **libero** is a 'free defender' or sweeper. From the
Italian *battitore libero* (literally 'free beater'), the term describes a
skilful defender who, in addition to 'sweeping up' the ball in
defence if necessary, is free to roam up and down the field helping
to build attacking moves, without the responsibility of having to
mark opposing players. Players are said to 'play' or 'operate' 'as
a *libero*' or 'in the *libero* role'. *See also* SWEEPER.

● links

Why are golf courses, especially those on low-lying ground by the
sea, called **links**? It has nothing to do with the links of a chain,
although a series of holes might be thought of as connected in a
kind of chain, with the green of one hole positioned next to the

WARFARE

Given that sport is essentially an activity in which one side contests aggressively against another, it is scarcely surprising that so much of its metaphorical texture derives from the language of combat, warfare and weaponry. This is particularly the case in team sports where one side **attacks** while the other **defends**. In football, for example, players **shoot** at goal, hoping to hit the **target**. **Shots** can also be **fired**, **rifled** or **volleyed**. Teams have **marksmen** who **lead the line**. Those without such a player lack **firepower**. Opposing teams **battle** for possession. Teams have **captains** and **midfield generals**. Attempts to win championships are **campaigns**. Basketball players can be described as **gunners**, quarterbacks throw **bombs**, a batsman can **shoulder arms**, a team's home ground can be a **fortress**.

tee of the next. In Scots usage, the word originally referred to undulating ground near the seashore, covered by coarse grass and sand dunes. Such ground was used for the first golf courses. The word ultimately comes from an Old English word *hlinc* meaning 'rising ground' or 'ridge'.

● lip

Lip is a term used in both golf and snooker and refers to roughly the same thing, the rim of the hole in one case and the very edge of the pocket in the other. If a golfer's putt **lips out** it hits the rim of the hole but fails to drop in: 'her seven-footer hit the cup and lipped out', 'Olazabal lipped out his par putt'.

● locker

In football and other sports, you will often hear commentators admiringly say of a player that he has, for example, 'everything in his **locker**' or 'that little bit of magic in his locker' or 'plenty left in his locker'. This refers to the repertoire of skills at the player's disposal, kept in reserve for use if necessary. It's an extended use of the old expression 'without a shot in the locker', meaning having no money or resources left, which derives from the idea of ammunition being kept in lockers on board sailing ships. *See also* SHOT IN THE BAG.

● lollipop

In the generally no-nonsense language of motor racing, **lollipop** is the surprisingly charming term for the sign on a stick held in front of the racing car during a pit stop. It says 'Brake' on one side, telling the driver to apply the brakes, and 'Go' on the other side, telling the driver when to shift into first gear and drive off.

● long-ball game

Rugby balls and American footballs may have a long shape, but in football a **long ball** is a long high pass upfield from a team's own half, which it is hoped will be latched onto by one of the forwards. To play the **long-ball game** is to adopt this direct style of play rather than building up an attack gradually with short passes. An indication of the somewhat negative opinion widely held of this tactic is the verb most often used as an alternative to 'play', that is, 'resort to'.

Everton played it short in midfield, probing for openings and using the wings, while Watford favoured the long-ball game – getting the ball into their opponents' penalty area by the quickest route. thefa.com, 8/4/03

See also ROUTE ONE.

● long hop

In cricket, a short-pitched ball (not fast or high enough to be a bouncer) that bounces up invitingly at a comfortable height for the batsman to smash to the boundary is known as a **long hop**, fitting nicely into the metaphorical theme that includes terms such as 'rabbit', 'bunny' and 'hutch'. *See also* BUNNY, HUTCH, RABBIT.

● loosener

A **loosener** is one of the first few deliveries of a bowler's spell, and the term tends to be used to partly excuse a poor piece of bowling, since the bowler is still 'loosening up'.

● lose the dressing room

This is not an indication of absent-mindedness but a sign of impending managerial departure. A manager really knows that his days are numbered when he **loses the dressing room**, that is, when he no longer has the confidence or the respect of the players:

The relationship had fractured, Ball had lost the dressing room, and there was no way back. Niall Quinn, Guardian, 14/10/05

● losingest

Grammatically suspect but commendably succinct, **losingest** is an Americanism meaning least successful or losing most often, as in 'the losingest team over the past decade' or 'the losingest pitcher in the NL'. *See also* WINNINGEST.

● love

A score of zero in tennis is referred to as **love**, whether this is zero points in a game, as in 'thirty–love', or zero games in a set, as in 'four games to love'. It is often suggested that this use originates from the French word *l'oeuf*, meaning 'egg', because of the resemblance between the oval shape of the numeral 0 and an egg. More likely, however, is that the term derives from the phrase 'play for love', meaning 'to play for the love of the game', that is, for nothing, not for money. Tabloid sub-editors are unable to resist headlines like 'Tennis Star's Love Match' or 'Love All on Tennis Court', whenever a story involves tennis players and romance.

● lower order

Not to be confused with the 'lower orders', a cricket side's **lower order** may, however, be regarded as occupying a level of **class** in the batting hierarchy below the specialist batsmen. The lower order consists of the batsmen coming in to bat roughly between numbers 8 and 11 in the batting order.

m

madison

Like the **keirin**, the **madison** is the name of a cycling event that
breaks into the consciousness of the wider sporting audience once
every four years at the Olympic Games. It is a long-distance track
race for teams of two riders, who take it in turns to sprint on the
track. Changeovers involve one rider grabbing his teammate's
hand and propelling him back onto the track. This type of race
originated at Madison Square Garden in New York City, hence
the name.

maiden

Why, in cricket, is an over in which no runs are scored by the batsman called a **maiden**? It might be supposed that there is some connection with the idea of the paper of the scorebook being unmarked
or 'virginal' in some way, but in fact the term comes from an old
use of *maiden* meaning 'unproductive'. The common use of the
word to mean 'happening for the first time' is also used in cricket in
expressions such as 'maiden century' or 'maiden Test match'.

maillot jaune

French for 'yellow jersey', the **maillot jaune** is the yellow jersey
worn by the race leader in the Tour de France. The colour of the

jersey is thought to derive from the French newspaper *L'Auto*, the Tour's founding sponsor, which introduced the idea of the race leader wearing a jersey the same colour as the yellow paper on which its pages were printed.

● makeable

Golf commentators are fond of describing a putt as **makeable**. This suggests that, while the putt's distance from the hole means that it is by no means routine, it is otherwise relatively straightforward and there is a good chance of it being holed.

● make a move/charge

In the latter stages of a golf tournament it is common to talk about certain players **making a move**, that is, scoring so well that their name begins steadily to move up the leaderboard and they challenge for the lead: 'Woods is well placed to make a move for the lead on Saturday', 'Els needs to make a move'. An even more aggressive push for the lead is described as **making a charge**: 'Karrie Webb will be looking to make a charge up the leaderboard.' Both phrases are used with words like 'be poised to', 'get into a position to' and 'be well placed to'. *See also* MOVING DAY.

● maker's name

When a batsman 'shows the **maker's name**' (or 'shows the bowler the maker's name') he plays a straight shot with a sound defensive technique in such a way that the manufacturer's logo on the face of the bat is clearly visible as the bat meets the ball.

● make the cut

To **make the cut** is to avoid being eliminated from a golf tournament at the midway point by getting a good enough score after two days. Only those players that achieve a given score or lower for the first 36 holes are permitted to play on in the final rounds. In general language, to **make the cut** means to be of a good enough standard or meet a certain qualification. *See also* CUT.

● make the turn

The halfway point on an 18-hole golf course is known as **the turn**: 'Mickelson was still one up at the turn.' To **make the turn** is to complete the 9th hole and move on to the 10th tee: 'Campbell birdied four holes on the front nine to make the turn at 32.' *See also* BACK NINE, FRONT NINE.

● make yourself big

In a one-to-one confrontation between a goalkeeper and a forward charging towards the goal, the keeper will try to impose himself physically and **make himself big**, standing not only tall but wide too and thereby reducing the size of the target:

The keeper stood his ground, made himself big, and O'Connor smacked his shot off his body.   dailyrecord.co.uk, 19/12/03

● man on

A phrase producing a Pavlovian response of mild panic in anyone who has ever played park football, '**man on!**' is a warning shouted to a teammate with the ball unaware of the fact that an opposition player is fast approaching from behind, requiring the teammate to take evasive action or pass the ball as quickly as possible.

● Maori sidestep

Maori sidestep is a choice piece of rugby slang associated with New Zealand's All Blacks side. As executed by gargantuan players charging forward with the ball, it involves no sidestep at all, but simply trampling straight over an opposing defender with the temerity to stand in the way.

● marathon not a sprint

A staple of the managerial interview is the observation that the baseball season (or football season, or whatever) 'is a **marathon not a sprint**'; in other words, a team's performance needs to be judged over the season as a whole, not merely on the first few results.

● marching orders

Another way of saying that a player has been sent off is to say that he has been given his **marching orders**:

Gronkjaer received his marching orders after clattering into Buruk, leaving Denmark to survive for an hour with only 10 men.
fifaworldcup.yahoo.com, 13/10/04

● mare

Footballers talk about having a **mare**, that is, a nightmare of a game, a 'shocker', when they perform embarrassingly badly: 'The right back had an absolute mare in the first half.'

● massive club

The term **massive club** seems to be reserved for currently under-achieving football clubs with an illustrious trophy-filled history and a large and loyal fan base, particularly a club no longer enjoying **top-flight** status. When Manchester City were struggling in the lower-division doldrums in the 1990s, United fans used to taunt their City rivals by chanting an ironic ditty called 'City are a Massive Club'. *See also* SLEEPING GIANT.

● maximum

In the language of snooker, a **maximum** (short for **maximum break**) is a score of 147, the highest possible score in a single break. *See also* ONE HUNDRED AND EIGHTY.

● mazy run

Going on **a mazy run**, a phrase relished by football commentators and journalists, is what used to be called dribbling, that is, jinking and zigzagging past a succession of defenders with the ball before shooting at goal or crossing to a teammate:

Giggs went on a mazy run through the middle and lifted the ball in for Hartson to head down. soccernet.com, 2/6/01

● meat in the sandwich

When horses are running close together in a race, a horse that is closed in from both sides by competitors may be described as the **meat in the sandwich**:

She had a slightly unlucky run at York. She was drawn between two horses and the one on her left went right, the one on her right went left, and she was the meat in the sandwich. Michael Jarvis, gg.com, 4/7/05

● meat of the bat

The centre of the blade of a cricket bat is sometimes referred to as the **meat of the bat**. *See also* MIDDLE, SWEET SPOT.

● medal

Medal can be used as a verb in sport, meaning to win a gold, silver or bronze medal, as in 'she's medalled at the last two World Championships' or 'he's hoping to medal in the 200 metres'. *See also* PODIUM FINISH.

● Mendoza line

In baseball, to have a batting average below .200 is to be hitting below the **Mendoza line**, which unofficially sets the acceptable standard for hitters in the major leagues. This benchmark for poor hitting is named after Mario Mendoza, a shortstop with the Pittsburgh Pirates, the Seattle Mariners and the Texas Rangers in the 1970s, who had a reputation as a poor batter. Mendoza's lifetime batting average was in fact .215 and it is sometimes this figure that is used to mark the level of the Mendoza line, though .200 is more common. The coining of the term is generally credited to the baseball player George Brett. In general American usage it can refer to a standard of just-acceptable mediocrity or respectability, as in 'his approval ratings hover below the political Mendoza line of 20 per cent' or 'a joke on the Mendoza line of good taste'.

● mercurial

A favourite adjective in the commentators' lexicon, **mercurial**, meaning 'lively and unpredictable' is generally applied to southern Europeans ('the mercurial Frenchman', 'the mercurial Italian') or gifted individualists ('the mercurial George Best', 'the mercurial Gascoigne').

● merry-go-round

There are two types of merry-go-round in football, the **managerial merry-go-round** (a cycle of managers being sacked, vacancies becoming available and appointments being made to fill them, all within a short period of time) and the **transfer merry-go-round** (the flurry of activity during one of the 'transfer windows' as players move between clubs).

● metronomic accuracy

The consistent, probing accuracy of such bowlers as Glenn McGrath, Shaun Pollock and Anil Kumble tends to attract the seemingly obligatory description of **metronomic**. It is difficult to find an article about McGrath in particular that fails to allude at some point to that regularly ticking device.

● Michelle

One of the more amusingly inventive pieces of cricketing slang is **Michelle**, as in Michelle Pfeiffer. What's the Hollywood star got to do with cricket? Well, she was in *Batman Returns*, which perhaps suggests a player striding out of the pavilion for his second innings. And the title of another of her films *What Lies Beneath* might call to mind the dangers lurking in a fifth-day wicket. In fact, the feat of a bowler taking five wickets in an innings is known as a 'five-for' or 'fifer', generally pronounced just like the actress's surname. According to the customary principles of rhyming slang, the rhyming word (Pfeiffer) is discarded and the non-rhyming element (Michelle) retained. *See also* FIFER.

● middle

In cricket, 'to **middle** it' is to hit the ball with the middle of the blade of the bat, playing the shot with perfect timing and maximum power. *See also* MEAT OF THE BAT, SWEET SPOT.

● midfield general

The great Hungarian footballer Ferenc Puskas may have been known as the Galloping Major, but every team hopes to have a **midfield general**. This is the term for a central midfielder, capable of strong tackles and accurate passes, who is able to stamp his authority on the pitch, controlling the pace of the game.

● military medium

An old-fashioned and rather disparaging term, **military medium** describes medium-pace bowling that while being steady and efficient is also innocuous and predictable.

● moonball

A very high lob in tennis is informally known as a **moonball**.

● morning glory

A racehorse that runs impressively in morning workouts but fails to reproduce the same level of performance on the racecourse is described as a **morning glory**, from the name of a climbing plant with trumpet-shaped flowers that close in the late afternoon.

● mountain to climb

The size of the task facing a player or team is often described as a **mountain to climb**, as in 'we have a mountain to climb if we are to avoid relegation' or 'once we'd gone two down we were left with a mountain to climb'. A pleasing variation was offered by Jurgen Klinsmann, the coach of the German national team, when in November 2005 he considered his side's prospects in the forthcoming World Cup: 'We have Mount Kilimanjaro in front of us. We started climbing it in August 2004.' *See also* BIG ASK.

● mouse

In boxing parlance, a **mouse** is a swollen bruise around a boxer's eye.

● mouth

Snooker can seem a somewhat mouth-fixated sport, with its **kisses**, **jaws** and **lips**. And, indeed, the pocket opening is often referred to as the **mouth** of the pocket.

● move the goalposts

In general usage, **moving the goalposts** is changing the previously agreed rules or conditions of a procedure after it has started, to the disadvantage of someone taking part in it. The metaphor suggests a football goal having its posts shifted closer together during the course of a match, making the goalmouth a narrower target.

● moving day

In a four-day golf tournament, **moving day** is the third day, usually a Saturday, when competitors make their move up the leaderboard standings, positioning themselves to win on the final day. Other competitors, of course, see their names move down the leaderboard as they slip out of contention.

After two days without wind at the Long Island links, the breeze picked up on 'moving day' and the scoring went through the roof.
bbc.co.uk, 19/6/04

See also MAKE A MOVE/CHARGE.

● **mudlark**

A racehorse that runs well on wet or heavy ground is known as a **mudlark**. The original mudlarks were people who made a living by scavenging in river mud for saleable objects. *See also* TOP OF THE GROUND.

● **mulligan**

In friendly games of golf a player who makes a mess of his tee shot, especially on the opening hole of a round, may sometimes be granted another go. This second drive, not counted on the scorecard, is known in the US as a **mulligan**. The origin of the term, dating from the 1940s, is not certain but it may derive from the name of a bottle containing a mixture of pepper-seeds and water, freely available on the bar in saloons, which could be added to a beer to spice it up.

● **MVP**

In various American sports such as baseball, American football and basketball, the title **MVP** (most valuable player) is awarded to the best player in a team or league. The term is also used in non-sporting contexts. For example, in business, the best-performing employee in a company might be named the company's MVP. *See also* DNF.

n

neck and crop

A batsman bowled **neck and crop** is bowled 'all ends up', comprehensively beaten by the delivery. A rather old-fashioned expression meaning 'completely or thoroughly', it was originally used in the context of a horse falling to the ground, the 'crop' here either being the rider's whip or (as a variant of *croup*) the horse's hindquarters.

Nelson

Nelson is a score of 111 by a team or an individual batsman, traditionally considered to be unlucky by superstitious English cricketers. Fearing the imminent fall of a wicket, the members of the batting side in the pavilion are supposed to ward off the bad luck by taking their feet off the ground until the score moves off the dreaded Nelson. The now-retired umpire David Shepherd was famous for hopping up and down until Nelson was passed. A score of 222 is known as **double Nelson**. The designation 'Nelson' is ingeniously derived from the fact that Lord Nelson had one eye, one arm and one leg. Ingenious but erroneous. Nelson, of course, had two legs.

● nervous nineties

The Nervous Nineties sounds a far less appealing decade than the Naughty Nineties, as the 1890s are often dubbed. The 1990s, perhaps? In fact, the **nervous nineties** is a term used in cricket for the period of a batsman's innings when he has a score between 90 and 99, and suddenly finds he is batting with much less fluency and confidence as he anxiously approaches his century:

Strauss had hit a bit of congestion in the 80s, but did away with the nervous 90s altogether as he went from 88 to 100 in the space of four balls bowled by Harbhajan. bbc.co.uk, 18/3/06

● never up, never in

Never up, never in is a near-proverbial adage of golf, commenting on the fact that a putt struck too softly to reach the hole has no chance of falling in.

● nick a goal

In baseball you can **steal a base** and in football you **nick a goal** (or **nick one**). The expression usually describes a goal scored on the counter-attack, after a team has spent most of a game defending:

That will be the game plan, to keep a clean sheet and nick a goal. Steven Gerrard, 5/4/05

Winning a game in this way is known as **nicking it**. In cricket, on the other hand, **nicking it** is what a batsman does when he gets a slight touch to the ball with the edge of his bat.

See also SMASH-AND-GRAB.

● nickel defense

In American football, a **nickel defense** is a defensive formation with an additional defensive back, making five in total. A nickel is, of course, a coin worth five cents. *See also* DIME DEFENSE.

● nightwatchman

In the language of cricket, much of the vocabulary of batting ('take guard', 'defend', 'put up the shutters', etc.) relates to the idea of protecting one's wicket. In the same metaphorical territory is the term **nightwatchman**, conjuring up an image of a man outside a little hut warming his hands by a glowing brazier. If a wicket falls a short time before the end of a day's play, it is common practice for a lower-order batsman, known in these circumstances as the nightwatchman, to be sent in to bat ahead of his usual place in the batting order, to protect a more skilled and valuable batsman from having to face the final overs of the day.

● no one likes us, we don't care

To the tune of Rod Stewart's hit 'Sailing', '**no one likes us, we don't care**' is the chant sung by the fans of Millwall football club, in spirited defiance of what the supporters believe to be an unfair and exaggerated reputation for hooliganism.

● nose

In the US, the narrowest winning margin in a horse race is a **nose**. In the UK, it's a short head. *See also* CANVAS, HEAD, LENGTH.

● not at the races

One sport will sometimes refer figuratively to another. After a particularly poor performance a football manager, say, will admit that his team was **not at the races**:

We've not been at the races away from home at times this season.
Stuart Pearce, Manchester City manager, 11/3/06

It's a variation on the idea of 'just not turning up', performing too far below par to compete.

See also CRICKET SCORE.

GOALSCORING

Scoring goals is frequently written about using metaphors of hunting and theft. Strikers are described as

predators

or goal-
poachers.

Chances are
taken.

Winners are
snatched to **steal**
the points.

Balls, crosses or passes are
seized upon or **snaffled**
by players who go on to score

Goals are
poached or **netted**.

A striker might
bag a brace
of goals

or even
plunder
a hat trick.

● not cricket

Behaviour can be described as **not cricket** if it is thought to be underhand or unsporting, contrary to the standards of fair play in which the game of cricket is traditionally supposed to be played.

● nothing ball

'The goal came out of a nothing ball launched into the box': in football-speak, a **nothing ball** is a disappointing or innocuous-looking pass, particularly when this subsequently leads to a goalscoring opportunity.

● nothing left in the tank

It may be said of an exhausted sportsman, at the end of his resources, that he has **nothing left in the tank**. As with the expression 'running on empty', there is the idea of a car that has all but run out of petrol:

Kipchoge said that because he had set a lot of the pace he had nothing left in the tank…'I had nothing left to give'. Middle East Online, 30/8/04

Paige hung in there, showing guts because he had nothing left in the tank by the 6th round. ringsidereport.com, 20/11/05

The phrase can also be used to convey the idea of giving your all, offering total effort and commitment on the field of play: 'We'll have nothing in the tank when we come off the pitch.'

● nuggety

In cricket, the adjective **nuggety** suggests toughness and determination, as in 'Thorpe was a nuggety batsman' and 'Andrew Strauss eked out a nuggety 129'.

● nurdle

Nurdle, a delightful word, is a term used in cricket to describe a batting style in which the batsman scores runs by nudging the ball gently into gaps between the fielders, as in 'Bell nurdled his way to 65' or 'Collingwood nurdles the ball into the leg side and picks up a single'.

● nutmeg

In football a player **nutmegs** an opponent when he kicks the ball through the other player's legs and then runs past to retrieve it. Why this cheeky manoeuvre is called a nutmeg isn't certain. Among various theories that have been advanced are suggestions that the term is rhyming slang for 'legs' or is an extension of 'nuts', slang for 'testicles'. Another possibility is that its use is related to an old meaning of *nutmeg*, 'to trick or deceive someone, especially in a way that makes them look foolish', one that has its origin in a 19th-century practice of carving fake nutmegs out of wood and selling them in place of real ones.

o

occupy the crease

In cricket, to **occupy the crease** is to bat defensively or cautiously with the principal aim of not getting out rather than necessarily scoring runs quickly:

[Gavaskar] could occupy the crease for long hours, with playing out time often more critical than scoring at a quick pace. Amit Varma, Observer, 19/3/06

oche

'Andy Fordham is on the oche': one of the odder words in the sporting lexicon, **oche** is the term for the line that darts players must stand behind when throwing. It is pronounced 'ockey' and indeed *hockey* used to be the more common written form of the word. Its origin isn't certain, though it may be related to the Old French word *ocher* meaning 'to cut a deep notch in something'. Another theory is that it derives from *hocks*, a slang word for feet.

ofer

While a 'fifer' is a success in cricket, an **ofer** is a failure in baseball. A player who does not score a hit in a game can be so described, with the following number indicating the number of at bats (that is, turns at batting) taken: 'He went ofer four' (or 'oh-for-four'). *See also* FIFER.

off

In a sentence like 'the cars are lined up on the grid, ready for the off' the **off** is, of course, the start of the race. But the word has another meaning in motor-racing slang. A car that accidentally leaves the track is said to have 'had an off':

Michael Schumacher suffered a big off in the closing minutes of Saturday practice. justracing.com, 27/12/04

Also worth noting as a common use of **off** in sportspeak is its appearance in phrases such as 'off-the-pitch incident', 'off-court distractions', 'off-track drama', 'off-the-oche problems' and so on.

off base

In American usage, to be **off base** is to be wrong or mistaken. In baseball, if a runner mistakenly steps off a base while the ball is in play, he is in danger of being put out. *See also* COVER ALL THE BASES, GET TO FIRST BASE, TOUCH BASE.

officiate

According to football commentators, referees **officiate**. It's an example of the slight pomposity that football-speak is curiously prone to now and then.

off the back

A cyclist who has gone **off the back** in a race is unable to keep pace with the main group of riders and is dropping behind.

off the bit/bridle

When, in the latter stage of a race, a jockey gives a racehorse its head to run as fast as it can, no longer restrained at all by the use of the reins and the bit in its mouth, it is said to be **off the bit** or **off the bridle**. *See also* ON THE BIT/BRIDLE.

● off the front

A cyclist who has gone **off the front** takes part in a breakaway from the main group of riders.

● off your own bat

To do something **off you own bat** is to do it of your own accord or without any help. This is a cricketing metaphor, referring to the runs that an individual batsman scores, perhaps in a situation where the better of two batsmen takes on the responsibility of scoring all the runs.

● on deck

In baseball, a batter who is **on deck** is next in the batting order, due to take his turn at the plate after the current batter. He is out of the dugout and waiting to bat, like a sailor waiting to report for duty on deck. *See also* IN THE HOLE.

● one hundred and eighty

A bellowed cry of '**one hundred and EIGHTY!**', gloriously reminiscent of the style of a Victorian fairground barker, is the customary way for a darts referee to announce a score of three treble 20s, the maximum possible score with three darts.

● one-on-one

A situation in which a footballer is bearing down on goal with only the goalkeeper to beat is known as a **one-on-one**. It doesn't seem to be used for any other two-player confrontations elsewhere on the pitch. American in origin, the term is also used in such sports as basketball and ice hockey.

onion bag

The netting of a football goal is sometimes humorously described as the **onion bag**, as in 'he put the ball in the onion bag'. This is particularly appropriate when you picture several footballs being carried onto the training ground in a net, resembling a string-bagful of onions.

on the bit/bridle

A racehorse still being held back by a jockey by the use of the reins and the bit in its mouth is said to be running **on the bit** or **on the bridle**. The idea is that once the jockey 'lets it go' the horse will quicken its pace. *See also* OFF THE BIT/BRIDLE.

on the bounce

On the bounce is the modish version of 'in a row', used to refer to a winning or losing streak, hence 'a run of three wins on the bounce', 'we've lost five home matches on the bounce' and 'we're chasing a fourth win on the bounce':

Rampant Barcelona claimed a record-breaking 12th win on the bounce with a 3–1 success at Cadiz last night. sundaymail.co.uk, 18/12/05

The phrase **on the spin** is also used: 'we've had nine wins on the spin', 'this is his sixth title on the spin'.

on the bubble

In American sport, to be **on the bubble** is to be on the verge of qualifying to compete in a tournament, or for the remainder of one. If, for example, on the second day of a four-day golf tournament a player completes his round with a score hovering around that likely to be necessary to 'make the cut', he is said to be 'on the bubble', poised in a kind of golfing limbo until he learns at the end of the day's play whether he is on the right or the wrong side of the cut-off score:

> *[Snedeker] made the turn at 3 over, playing steady golf until a bogey 5 on the 18th put him on the bubble.* usaga.org, 10/4/04

The expression aptly suggests the precarious position of a player waiting to learn his fate in this way: not only is it uncertain in which direction anything on the slippery surface of a bubble will slide off, but a bubble is fragile and apt to burst at any time. The phrase is also used when discussing, as the end of the season approaches, which players are below but close to the 125th position in the PGA Tour money list. This is significant because it is only the top 125 money-winners who are guaranteed to retain their Tour cards for the following year, giving them exemption from qualifying for that year's tournaments:

> *Rocco Mediate, last week's man on the bubble at 125, also created some valuable breathing room with a move to 120.* pgatour.com, 2/11/05

But the phrase is not confined to golf. In US college basketball, for instance, teams waiting to discover whether they have been selected to compete in the NCAA championship are described as 'on the bubble'. *See also* MAKE THE CUT.

● on the rivet

It sounds painful, and it probably is. A cyclist described as **on the rivet** is riding extremely hard. Leather saddles used to have a rivet on the front, just where you sit on a bike when making an all-out effort.

● on the ropes

The expression **on the ropes**, meaning 'in a desperate position, on the verge of defeat', comes from the boxing ring. A boxer forced back against the ropes by his opponent's blows is often close to defeat.

● out-and-out striker

Describing a particular striker as an **out-and-out** one emphasizes that you are talking about a specialist goalscorer, in contrast to a forward who plays **in the hole**, linking play between midfield and attack:

Newcastle remain in the market for an out-and-out striker with Real Madrid's Michael Owen topping their list. independent.co.uk, 27/8/05

See also TARGET MAN.

● out for the count

If a boxer is knocked to the ground and unable to rise to his feet within the referee's count of ten, he is said to be **out for the count**. The phrase is used in everyday language to describe someone sleeping deeply, unconscious or perhaps beaten in a contest.

● out of left field

In baseball, left field is the part of the playing area to the left of the batter when facing the pitcher. To the batter's right is right field. In the 1920s New York Yankees fans crowded into the seats behind the right-field fence of the Yankee Stadium because the right field was not only where the great Babe Ruth (a left-hander) hit his home runs but also where he usually fielded. Deliberately choosing to buy tickets for the left-field seats seemed rather perverse or idiotic. This is traditionally thought to be the origin of the expression **out of left field**, used to describe something unusual, unexpected or unorthodox.

● own goal

Figuratively, to score an **own goal** is to take an action that turns out to be harmful to your own interests. In football, of course, scoring an own goal is accidentally striking or deflecting the ball into your own team's net, giving a goal to the opposing side.

p

pace

Pace is the usual term in football (often preceded by 'blistering' or 'searing') for the speed with which players can run: 'Johnson tormented the Liverpool defence all game with his searing pace.' A team may 'have pace in abundance' or 'lack pace at the back'. Indeed, **pace** seems to be the preferred term generally in sport. In cricket, for example, deliveries are hurled down the pitch 'with pace' by fast bowlers, otherwise known as 'pace bowlers' or 'pacemen'. Racehorses and athletes are either 'up with' or 'off' the pace.

pacer

Pacer is a recent journalistic alternative to **pace bowler** or **paceman** as a term for a fast bowler, used especially in Pakistan. The word is more generally familiar in the modified form 'medium-pacer'.

paddock

Some motor-racing terminology originates in the language of the racecourse. An example is the word *paddock*, which in horse racing is the enclosure where the horses are paraded before the start of a race. The **paddock** at a motor-racing track is the area behind the pits where the racing teams park their trucks and motor homes and where the racing cars are worked on before a race. There is not a blade of grass in sight. *See also* POLE POSITION.

paint the black

To **paint the black** (or simply to **paint**) in baseball is to throw a pitch that passes right over the edge of the strike zone. 'Paint' suggests the artistry of high-quality pitching and 'black' refers to the black border around the home plate. *See also* IN THE PAINT

pair

In cricket, a batsman who is out for a score of nought (a 'duck') in both his innings in a match is said to have got a **pair**. This is short for a **pair of spectacles**, not a slight on the hapless batsman's eyesight, but because 0–0 resembles a pair of glasses. A batsman who has got a duck in his first innings is said to be 'on a pair' as he walks out to bat a second time. *See also* DUCK, GOLDEN PAIR.

palooka

The US term **palooka** refers to a boxer of limited ability, often an older fighter with his best days in the ring behind him. The origin of the word, first recorded in print in the 1920s, is uncertain. *See also* HAM AND EGGER, TOMATO CAN.

par

In golf, **par** is the standard number of strokes a first-class player is expected to take for a particular hole or course. The term dates from the late 19th century, ultimately deriving from the 16th-century sense 'equality of value or standing', from Latin *equal*. **Par** can also be used as a verb, meaning 'to score par': 'He parred the first five holes.'

● par for the course

The expression **par for the course**, meaning 'what is to be expected in the circumstances', alludes to the standard score a good golfer should expect on a particular course.

● park

Park is the footballers' word for football pitch, as in 'our keeper was the busiest man on the park'. To play another team 'off the park' is to outplay them. To 'kick them off the park' is to attempt to beat them by the systematic use of fouls.

● passing shot

A **passing shot** in tennis is one that you hit past your opponent and beyond his or her reach.

● pavilion

In the language of cricket, the **pavilion**, the building at a cricket ground where the players get changed and wait to bat, can also symbolize the end of a batsman's innings as he is 'sent back to the pavilion':

Muttiah Muralitharan had Trescothick caught behind for 27, and 10 minutes later Strauss followed his opening partner back to the pavilion when he was run out on 30. sportal.com.au, 26/5/06

See also IN THE CLUBHOUSE.

● peg

A footballer's leg or foot is sometimes described as his **peg**, but curiously it is much more likely to refer to the left one than the right one: 'a young midfielder with a quality left peg', 'he scored the winner with his left peg'. **Peg** is also a rather old-fashioned word for a cricket stump, as in 'the ball clipped the off peg'.

Ornithology

Sport boasts a veritable aviary of bird-related terms.

Golf leads the way with its **birdies**, **eagles** and **albatrosses**,
not to mention its **bird's nest** lies and **quail high** shots.
Cricket has its **ducks** and
baseball its **ducks on the pond** and **dying quail**.
Racehorses can be said to be **catching pigeons**.

A **goose egg** is an unwelcome score in American sport.
Football teams have left and right **wings**.

And, of course, there is the classic footballing cliché
sick as a parrot, though few players actually say this nowadays.
Many sports team names are inspired by the names of birds,
especially in the US. Major league baseball teams include
the St Louis **Cardinals**, the Toronto **Blue Jays**
and the Baltimore **Orioles**.
American football in the NFL is played by teams with
names such as the Atlanta **Falcons**, the Baltimore **Ravens**,
the Philadelphia **Eagles**, the Seattle **Seahawks** and
the Arizona **Cardinals**.
Birds of prey figure, too, in the names of British rugby teams like
the Newcastle **Falcons** and the Neath-Swansea **Ospreys**.
Finally, the nicknames of many British football clubs have an
ornithological theme, including
the **Magpies** (Newcastle United, Notts County),
the **Owls** (Sheffield Wednesday), the **Canaries** (Norwich City),
the **Seagulls** (Brighton),
the **Robins** (Bristol City, Swindon Town and others),
the **Bluebirds** (Cardiff City) and
the **Eagles** (Crystal Palace).

● peloton

In a cycling road race, the **peloton** is the main pack of riders.
Like many cycling terms, it's a French word, literally meaning
'small ball' or 'small detachment of soldiers', and is related to the
English word *platoon*.

● percentage shot

In sports such as cricket, tennis, golf and basketball, a **percentage
shot** is a shot a player chooses to play in a given situation that
has the least likelihood of error:

*Owing to the steepness of the bounce in Australia, the sweep has not
been a percentage shot in this series.* telegraph.co.uk, 29/12/02

A low-risk, safety-first style of play can be described as **playing
the percentages** or **percentage play**.

● perfect game

A **perfect game** is a game of baseball in which a pitcher retires
every batter he faces in nine innings, with no batter reaching
base.

● pie chucker

Pie chucker (or **pie thrower**) is a derogatory expression used
in cricket for a bowler of poor-quality deliveries. Like 'buffet
bowling', the term is an example of the cricketing gastro-metaphor.
See also BUFFET BOWLING.

● pinch hitter

In baseball, a **pinch hitter** is a hard-hitting batter who is put
into bat, replacing another player in the batting order, in a critical
situation during a game. The term derives from *pinch*, meaning an
emergency or desperate situation, a 'tight spot'. Figuratively,
anyone substituting for another in a crisis can be described as a

pinch hitter. The term has been borrowed by cricket but has a rather different meaning, describing a big-hitting lower-order batsman who is promoted higher up the batting order to score runs quickly, especially in a one-day match.

ping

In horse racing, to **ping** a fence is to jump it really well, to 'nail' it:

It was an easy ride, he pinged the last two fences when he just stood off and he loves racing. Conor O'Dwyer, on winning the Cheltenham Gold Cup on War of Attrition, 17/3/06

A rugby referee **pings** a player or team when he penalizes them for an infringement of the rules, as in 'Jones was pinged for holding onto the ball'. The word comes from the high-pitched sound as the referee blows his whistle.

pin high

'Pin long' would perhaps be more logical, but **pin high** is a golfing expression describing a ball hit to the green that is exactly the right distance but that comes to rest to one side of the flag (the pin): 'The ball ended up pin high, a foot to the left.'

pipe-opener

Pipe-opener is a horse-racing term for an early-season race, or a training run in preparation for a race, in both cases a spell of exercise intended to get air into the horse's lungs, to 'blow away the cobwebs'.

pits

Why are the **pits** on a motor-racing circuit, where cars are brought in for maintenance and refuelling during a race, so-called? Like 'dugout' in football, the term originally referred to an area that was actually below ground level. Introduced at the Targa Florio race in Sicily in 1908, the original pits were dug by the side of the track, so that mechanics could replace the detachable rims of the car tyres. **Pit** can also be used as a verb, meaning 'to come into the pits'. An unrelated use of the word in sport occurred in 1981 when John McEnroe, during one of his familiar outbursts over a disputed line-call, famously called a Wimbledon umpire 'the pits of the world'. *See also* DUGOUT.

● plant

A **plant** in snooker is a shot that involves hitting the cue ball onto one ball, which in turn (and as intended) strikes another ball into a pocket.

● play a few shots

Play a few shots is a rather understated cricketing expression used of a batsman prepared to play in a positive way and hit boundaries, perhaps taking a few risks, either following a period of relative circumspection or despite the generally defensive approach that the match situation demands:

I was enjoying my time at the crease after I'd got to about 60, which was when I started to try to play a few shots and cleared the ropes a couple of times. Michael Vaughan, England cricket captain, 21/11/04

● play ball

Colloquially, to **play ball** is to cooperate with someone. The idea is that you can't play a ball game without other people.

● play catch-up

A team or individual that falls behind early on in a match, especially by a significant margin, may spend much of the time trying to get back on level terms or, to use the stock phrase, **playing catch-up**:

Some bad double faults and errors meant I was playing catch-up in the third set. Andy Murray, 5/1/06

The term **catch-up rugby** is common:

I'm disappointed because we started so badly and we had to play catch-up rugby. Jake White, South Africa rugby coach, 26/11/05

● play hardball

In business or politics, **playing hardball** is being tough, ruthless or aggressive in one's dealings or tactics. 'Hardball' here refers to the sport of baseball, when contrasted with softball.

● playmaker

A **playmaker** in football is a player, usually an attacking midfielder like Paul Gascoigne or Zinedine Zidane, with the ability to bring teammates into attacking positions and help set up scoring opportunities. The term is also used in other sports such as basketball and American football.

● plumb

In the context of a cricket match, **plumb** is always used with reference to a decision as to whether a batsman is out LBW (leg before wicket) and means 'indisputable, obvious', as in 'he was plumb LBW' (or simply 'he was plumb') or 'that was plumb'. *See also* STONEWALL.

● poacher

A **poacher** (or **goal poacher**) is a striker who specializes in scoring goals from close range, usually inside the penalty box. The term occupies the same metaphorical territory as **nick a goal** and **smash-and-grab**.

With just two minutes remaining Inzaghi showed his poacher's instinct by reacting quickest to turn home a loose ball in the six-yard box and send the San Siro wild. football.co.uk, 5/4/06

● podium finish

A **podium finish** (or **podium place**) is when a racing driver finishes a race in first, second or third place and gets to stand on the winners' podium and spray all that champagne around. It is the motor racing equivalent of an athlete **medalling**. Drivers finishing in the top three also talk about 'getting a podium'.

Felipe Massa was a happy man after bagging his first Formula One podium finish with a mature drive in Sunday's European Grand Prix. planet-f1.com, 7/5/06

Despite giving my all throughout the race it was not enough to get a podium. Kimi Raikkonen, 7/5/06

● pole position

Pole position is the first place on the starting grid, on the front row and on the inside the first bend, given to the driver with the fastest qualifying time. A driver can also be said to be **on pole**, as in 'Raikkonen is on pole for the German Grand Prix'. The term has its origin in horse racing, where a pole marked the starting position (a favourable one) closest to the inside fence of the racecourse. In general usage, to be in **pole position** is to have an advantageous starting position. *See also* PADDOCK.

● pooch kick

In American football, a **pooch kick** (also known as a **squib kick**) is a low, flat kick-off that can lead to the ball bouncing unpredictably once it hits the ground.

● pop

Football players and managers sometimes use the word **pop** to mean a shot on goal, especially a speculative one from some distance out: 'Deco had a pop at goal from 25 yards out', 'Mellor tries a pop from distance'.

● pouch

Cricket journalists sometimes use **pouch** to mean 'take a catch', an alternative to the more common (and semantically similar) 'pocket':

Muralitharan skies a steepling catch that is safely pouched by Plunkett.
bbc.co.uk, 26/5/06

● pound for pound

Boxing fans enjoy debating the questions 'who is (or was) the best boxer, **pound for pound**?'. In other words, if you imagine that boxers in different weight divisions were actually the same size and could fight one another, who would emerge as the champ? Many people rate five-time world middleweight champion Sugar Ray Robinson as the greatest pound-for-pound boxer of all time.

● proven goalscorer

When a football manager needs to strengthen his team in the goalscoring department by buying a striker, he is often said to be looking for a **proven goalscorer**, that is, an experienced player with an impressive track record of scoring goals, as opposed to, say, a young prospect with great potential but limited experience at the highest level.

● provider

Provider is a football commentators' word to describe a player who lays on a goalscoring opportunity for a teammate. When the player already has a goal of his own under his belt, the phrase 'turn provider' is useful: 'Andy Rodgers opened the scoring for Dumbarton with an unstoppable shot from 12 yards before turning provider for the second goal.' *See also* ASSIST.

● pull the trigger

In football, as a player makes contact with the ball in shooting at goal, he can be said to **pull the trigger**, particularly if the shot is blocked or thwarted. The phrase joins not only 'shoot' but also an assortment of other contributions to football's firearm-related vocabulary, such as 'rifle', 'volley', 'fire' and 'blast':

Great work from Tobias Linderoth teed-up Campbell from the centre of the penalty area, but as he pulled the trigger, Aaron Hughes' challenge just sent the ball wide for a corner. fs.football365.com, 3/4/04

● pump fake

You **pump fake** in basketball when you pretend to shoot for the basket but don't release the ball so that the defender will prematurely jump to block the ball, leaving you free to take a shot unchallenged. The term is also used for a similar manoeuvre in American football, in which the quarterback fakes a forward pass.

● Punch-and-Judy hitter

A **Punch-and-Judy hitter** in baseball is a batter who, though he tends to hit the ball rather softly, does so for well-placed singles.

● puncher's chance

Although the odds are on a technically superior boxer beating a less accomplished opponent, there is always the chance that a good punch could be a knockout blow, hence the term **a puncher's chance**. A similar idea is found in the old boxing adage that 'the last thing a fighter loses is his punch'.

He is a capable journeyman at best with no more than a puncher's chance against the towering Ukrainian. boxingscene.com, 2/9/05

The expression is used in other sports too, when discussing the possibility of an underdog defeating a stronger opponent:

Fernando Gonzalez went on to Court One for yesterday's quarter-final believing he had a puncher's chance of victory over Roger Federer.
Independent, 30/6/05

● put up the shutters

Batsmen are said to **put up the shutters** in a cricket match when they begin to bat purely defensively, usually in order to avoid the risk of losing wickets, and play for a draw. The metaphor carries the notion that business is effectively closed for the day, together with a sense that each batsman is barricading the path to his wicket. *See also* CLOSE THE DOOR.

● put your hand up

If as a sportsman you **put your hand up**, you take responsibility when the need arises. The expression comes from the idea of raising your hand to volunteer for something.

It's satisfying to put your hand up when it matters and do the things the team require as a batter and as a leader. Ricky Ponting, 15/8/05

This side has a lot of character. When we need someone to put a performance in, over a period of time now someone has put their hand up and done it. Andrew Flintoff, 15/11/05

See also STEP UP TO THE PLATE.

q

quail high

Eagles and **albatrosses** are not the only birds in the golfing lexicon. A poor shot hit **quail high** is one that supposedly resembles the flight of a startled quail, flying very low and level to the ground. *See also* DYING QUAIL.

quality

'A quality goal from a quality player': so the football commentator John Motson famously described a Tony Currie goal for Sheffield United in 1977. **Quality** (on its own, not modified by 'good', 'high' or 'top') is what the best teams and players have in abundance and the poor ones conspicuously lack:

It was a quality ball from Nicky Hunt to set up El-Hadji Diouf for the equaliser. Sam Allardyce, Bolton Wanderers manager, 15/9/05

There was a lack of quality from my players out there today. Jim Gannon, Stockport County manager, 1/3/06

quarterback

The **quarterback** in American football is the player who directs and coordinates the team's attacking play. He gets his name from the fact that he lines up behind the centre and is half as far back as the halfback. The term is sometimes borrowed to describe a corresponding role in other sports:

Beckham, removed from his quarterback role in the centre of midfield, was restored to what many people consider his natural position as a wide receiver. telegraph.co.uk, 9/10/05

It can also be used in non-sporting contexts, referring to the person who gives direction and leadership in a particular situation.

● quick

In cricket, **quick** can be used as a noun, especially in the plural, to refer to a fast bowler: 'It's time to bring the quicks back on.'

r

rabbit

The term **rabbit** is used in cricket to describe a lower-order
batsman, typically one of the specialist bowlers, who is particularly
hopeless at batting. *See also* BUNNY, FERRET.

rabbit punch

A **rabbit punch** is a sharp, chopping blow to the back of the
neck, an illegal punch in boxing because it is so dangerous. The
name comes from the similar technique used by hunters and
gamekeepers to kill rabbits.

raise the bar

'Roger Federer has raised the bar in men's tennis', it is routinely
said these days. Outstanding competitors, whose achievements
raise the standard of their sport to a new high level are often
described by their rivals, with rueful admiration, as having **raised
the bar**. The phrase (derived from high jumping and pole
vaulting) has been used habitually in recent years to evaluate the
performances of such other sporting figures as the golfer Tiger
Woods, the cyclist Lance Armstrong and, inevitably perhaps, the
pole vaulter Yelena Isinbayeva.

There is no doubt Chelsea have raised the bar. It is up to us to accept the challenge and do something about it. Alex Ferguson, manchesteronline.co.uk, 11/5/05

● red mist

When players lose their temper and resort to aggressive tackles or even fisticuffs, the commentators' cliché **red mist** is never far away. And what does this red mist invariably do? It 'descends'.

Red mist descended on the JJB Stadium as an explosive encounter saw both sides finish the game with 10 men. itv-football.co.uk, 15/3/06

See also HANDBAGS.

● regroup

To **regroup**, in a sporting context, is to regain confidence and resolve after a defeat or other setback, to prepare mentally to come back and compete with renewed effort. This usage is an extension of the idea of a military force reorganizing itself after being scattered by the enemy. **Regroup** is part of the stock vocabulary of defeat: it is what you have to do when you lose, the modern sportsman's equivalent of picking yourself up, dusting yourself down and starting all over again. Although it may appear to make more sense to talk about a team regrouping, the word can equally well be applied to an individual too.

We've got the one-day series now and that will help us to regroup and get people fit for the last two Tests, which I haven't given up on. Nasser Hussain, England cricket captain, following his team's crushing defeat by Australia in the Ashes series, 1/12/02

After being stunned by Mayer's quick start, Henman regrouped, reducing the errors on his own serve and gradually exerting pressure on the German's own service games. bbc.co.uk, 3/5/04

● repêchage

Every four years, television viewers following the Olympic Games
have the opportunity to become reacquainted with some esoteric
items of sporting terminology. One of these is **repêchage**. In
rowing, fencing, cycling and some other sports, this is the term for
a heat in which the runners-up in earlier heats compete against
one another and so get a second chance to qualify for the next
stage of the competition or the final. *Repêchage* comes from a
French word meaning 'fish out, rescue'.

● result

In sport, **the result** of a contest is, of course, the final score or
placing. But **a result** is a different matter and usually means a win:
'with a bit more luck we could well have got a result', 'we need to
get a result at Blackburn on Saturday'. The slightly qualified
version **any kind of result** simply means not losing, so could be
a draw: 'We'll do well to get any kind of result against this side.'

● ride the pine

To **ride the pine** (or **ride the bench** or 'shine the pine') is to
sit on the bench as a substitute. Pine is the traditional material
for benches in the dugout. *See also* BENCH, BENCH WARMER, SHINE
THE PINE.

● right off the bat

You do something **right off the bat** when you to do it straight
away or at the very beginning. Unlike the British idiom **off your
own bat** (deriving from cricket), this is an American expression
alluding to the instant a baseball is struck by the bat.

● rip

To **give the ball a rip** (especially **a real rip**) is, in cricket slang,
to impart a lot of spin on it, so that it turns after pitching more
than usual.

rock

Basketball players sometimes refer to the ball by the somewhat macho term **rock**, as in 'give me the rock' or 'shoot the rock'. To **dish the rock** is to pass the ball to another player.

rock up

Rock up is an Australian expression, meaning (but much cooler-sounding than) 'turn up or arrive', as in 'England will rock up to Old Trafford with their confidence sky-high'. Popular with cricketers, it is often used when warning of complacency, to scotch the idea that all a team has to do is turn up and they will be successful.

The focus this morning was probably all on our batting, and we just thought we would rock up and take the two wickets quite quickly and get back into the hut and start batting. Mickey Arthur, South Africa cricket coach, 27/12/05

I think even Shane would agree he can't just put his hand up and say 'I want to play in the World Cup' then just rock up for the first game. Ricky Ponting, 12/1/06

rope-a-dope

Rope-a-dope is the term for a boxing tactic of leaning back on the ropes of the boxing ring in order to conserve your strength and encourage your opponent to exhaust himself throwing repeated but ineffective punches, before eventually launching a counter-attack of your own. Muhammad Ali coined the term and it was the technique famously employed by him against George Foreman in the 'Rumble in the Jungle' world title fight in 1974. *See also* RUMBLE IN THE JUNGLE.

Route One

Route One is football slang for the most direct route to goal, more generally known as the 'long-ball game'. Rather than

A FEAST OF SPORT

Sport terminology serves up a hamper full
of terms relating to food and drink.
Imagine all this laid out for a picnic:
bagels, breadsticks, cans of corn,
cheese, cherries, fried eggs,
goose eggs, grand salami,
meat in the sandwich,
all washed down with
champagne.
The gastronomic theme continues with
buffet bowling, cup of coffee,
dunk, ham-and-egger,
ham and egging,
high cheese, jaffa, lollipop,
meat of the bat,
nutmeg, onion bag,
pie chucker
and
tomato can.

building up an attack from the back with a succession of short passes, a team will hoof the ball upfield roughly in the direction of one of the forwards. The term derives from the 1970s TV quiz show *Quiz Ball*, in which a contestant could choose 'route one' to goal, which entailed answering a single difficult question as opposed to, say, 'route four' which required the contestant to answer four easier questions. *See also* LONG-BALL GAME.

● Row Z

A ball that is kicked (or 'booted') into **Row Z** is deposited into the back of the stand, as far away from the pitch as possible. This is a football commentator's favourite phrase for describing a taking-no-chances clearance or a wildly inaccurate and overhit shot on goal.

● Roy of the Rovers stuff

The long-running British comic strip *Roy of the Rovers* depicted the footballing exploits of Melchester Rovers' star player Roy Race. Whenever a young player (especially a local boy) produces a dazzling performance or a team conjures up an extraordinary result against the odds, commentators and journalists are likely to reach for the cliché 'real **Roy of the Rovers stuff**':

Manchester City's 4–3 victory over Spurs at White Hart lane in the FA Cup after trailing 3–0 at half-time and down to 10 men truly was Roy of the Rovers stuff. Robert Philip, telegraph.co.uk, 7/2/04

● rub of the green

In sport, if a player or team gets the **rub of the green**, they have a piece of good fortune that gives them an advantage. The idiom comes from golf, where it refers specifically to a player's ball being accidentally deflected or stopped by an outside agency (for example, bouncing off a tree or hitting a spike mark), though not necessarily in a way that offers assistance to the player.

● Rumble in the Jungle

The **Rumble in the Jungle** was the promotional nickname, coined by Muhammad Ali, given to the world heavyweight title fight between Ali and George Foreman, which took place in Kinshasa, Zaire (now the Democratic Republic of the Congo) on 30 October 1974. The challenger Ali knocked out the champion Foreman in the eighth round, thus becoming world champion for the second time. This fight is the subject of both Norman Mailer's book *The Fight* (1975) and the documentary film *When We Were Kings* (1996). *See also* ROPE-A-DOPE, THRILLA IN MANILA, WAR ON THE SHORE.

● run and gun

Run-and-gun basketball is an attacking style of play that involves making fast breaks from defence and shooting often. The term is also used as a verb:

The Mavericks play a wide-open style with plenty of running and gunning. usatoday.com, 21/2/02

See also GUNNER.

● run-in

The final series of fixtures at the end of the season, which will decide whether a particular team wins a title or is promoted or relegated, is known as the **run-in**: 'it isn't an easy run-in', 'Rovers play all their fellow-strugglers in the run-in'. The term comes from horse racing, describing the final part of a race after the horses have jumped the last fence.

● run interference

In American football **running interference** is blocking a player from the opposing team to clear the way for a teammate carrying the ball. The phrase has passed over into general usage in American English. If you **run interference** for someone you help them by dealing with a problem for them or distracting attention away from them.

● run the clock down

Running the clock down (also called, in American English, **running out the clock** or **killing the clock**) is a time-wasting tactic used near the end of a game in many sports, including football, rugby, basketball and American football. This is when a team will deliberately use up as much of the remaining playing time as possible while retaining possession of the ball in order to deny the opposing team any opportunity to score and so protect a narrow lead:

That should have been it but as the game moved into injury time County attempted to run the clock down near the corner flag and lost possession. winningisnteverything.net, 18/1/06

The Eagles regained the ball with 1:03 left and appeared to be ready to run out the clock. sportsillustrated.cnn.com, 4/2/05

See also TAKE A KNEE.

● Russian linesman

Mention the words **Russian linesman** to any English football fan and they will immediately think of the 1966 World Cup final and Geoff Hurst's disputed goal. In extra time, with the score 2–2, Hurst fired a shot at the West German goal. The ball bounced down off the underside of the crossbar and out again. The question was, had the ball crossed the line? The Swiss referee Gottfried Dienst was unsure and it was only after consulting his linesman Tofik Bakhramov that he awarded England the goal. The so-called Russian linesman has had a cherished place in English footballing folklore ever since. Although he was from the Soviet Union, Bakhramov wasn't in fact Russian at all. Born in Baku, he should have been remembered as the Azerbaijani linesman.

S

safety

Safety on the snooker table is defensive play designed to leave your opponent little opportunity to pot balls by making sure the cue ball is left in a position that makes this difficult: 'a brilliant safety shot from Ebdon', 'his safety was superb'.

saved by the bell

The common phrase **saved by the bell** is used to refer to someone being rescued from an awkward or unpleasant situation in the nick of time by some timely intervention or interruption. It originates from a boxer being saved from being counted out by the ringing of a bell to indicate the end of a round:

A left hook from British boxer Henry Cooper floored Cassius Clay at Wembley in 1963. But Clay was saved by the bell and went on to triumph over Cooper. bbc.co.uk, 13/5/04

Say it ain't so, Joe

Baseball player 'Shoeless' Joe Jackson was banned from the sport for his alleged involvement in the infamous 'Black Sox' scandal of 1919, in which Jackson and seven other Chicago White Sox players were accused of conspiring to throw that year's World Series in return for bribes. According to baseball folklore, after

Jackson gave his testimony at the ensuing trial, a tearful boy approached his idol outside the courthouse and implored him to **'Say it ain't so, Joe!'**

scalp

In sport, to claim a **scalp** means to defeat an opponent in a knockout tournament, particularly one of the top players or teams, as in the headlines 'Orient Claims Premiership Scalp' or 'Murray Eyes Hewitt Scalp'. In cricket, to claim a **scalp** is to take a wicket, especially that of a notably good batsman ('a prized scalp'):

[Plunkett] had Michael Vandort brilliantly caught by Paul Collingwood in the gully with his third ball and three deliveries later claimed the prized scalp of Sri Lankan captain Mahela Jayawardene. sportinglife.com, 25/5/06

schoolboy howler

'A schoolboy howler by goalkeeper Oliver Kahn cost Bayern Munich an almost certain victory', began one match report in February 2004. **Schoolboy howler** is the quaintly old-fashioned stock phrase used by commentators and journalists to describe an elementary (and often amusing) mistake, especially one made by a goalkeeper or defender. Less common variations are 'schoolboy error' and 'schoolboy defending'.

scoreless

Although 0–0 is unquestionably a score, the word **scoreless** is sometimes used by football commentators as an alternative to 'goalless': 'We've played forty minutes and the match is still scoreless.' In other words, neither side has yet scored.

scoresheet

While it has no physical existence, the **scoresheet** (as in 'Lampard was soon on the scoresheet') is a popular metaphor for goalscoring. Why use one word ('score') when you can use four ('be' – or 'get' – 'on the scoresheet') or even six ('get your name on the scoresheet')? *See also* CLEAN SHEET.

● scramble

In golfing jargon, **scrambling** is salvaging a reasonable score on a hole despite first getting yourself into trouble: 'he chipped out from the trees and scrambled a par', 'she scrambled a bit on the back nine'.

● scrimmage

In a game of American football a **scrimmage** is a sequence of play between the two teams beginning with the snap (when the ball is put into play by being passed backwards). *Scrimmage*, dating from the 15th century, is an older word than the rugby equivalent *scrummage*, and is a variant of the word *skirmish*.

● seed

Why are the ranked competitors in sports tournaments, for example in tennis, known as **seeds**? Tournament organizers often assign places in the draw to the stronger players or teams who, based on their ability and recent form, are thought likely to reach the final stages. The intention is to keep the best competitors apart so that they don't play each other until the later rounds. The top-ranked player or team is known as the 'top seed'. There is an allusion to the idea of sowing or planting seeds a suitable distance apart so that they will thrive.

● sell a dummy

In rugby and football, you **sell** someone **a dummy** when you wrong-foot them by feigning a pass or kick. From the same verbal stable are expressions like 'can't buy a goal' and 'give the ball away cheaply'. *See also* BUY A GOAL, CHEAPLY.

● serve and volley

Serve and volley is a tennis term for a style of play that involves charging to the net immediately after serving, in order to be in a good position to volley the opposing player's return. *See also* CHIP AND CHARGE.

● set piece

In football, a **set piece** (also called a **set play**) is an opportunity for a team to score from a manoeuvre that can be practised on the training ground, such as a free kick or corner: 'Newcastle struggled to cope with Everton's aerial power at set pieces.'

● seventh-inning stretch

A tradition at baseball games is for spectators to stand up between the two halves of the seventh inning to stretch their legs, known as the **seventh-inning stretch**. The baseball anthem 'Take Me Out to the Ball Game' is often sung during this interval. According to a famous story, the origin of this custom was an occasion on which President William Taft rose from his seat during the seventh inning of a game in 1910, but in fact the custom appears to predate this (possibly apocryphal) episode by at least forty years.

● sexy

Ruud Gullit, on his appointment as manager of Newcastle United football club in 1998, promised to bring **sexy** football to the North East, that is, that his side's playing style would be attractive, exciting and attacking. From time to time, the adjective is applied to other sports. In February 2006 Wales rugby coach Mike Ruddock talked about his desire for his side to play 'sexy rugby'.

● shake and bake

A player who **shakes and bakes** (or **shakes 'n' bakes**) on a basketball court is playing to the gallery and indulging in ostentatiously showy play, often involving flamboyantly skilful dribbles and moves. The term takes its name from the proprietary name of a food coating mix called Shake 'N Bake. *See also* SHOWBOATING.

● shine the pine

To **shine the pine** is to sit on the bench as a substitute:

[Dallaglio] can expect to shine the pine on the replacements' bench for a while yet. Guardian, 6/2/06

Pine is the traditional material for benches in the dugout. Interestingly, this is one of those rhyming expressions (like basketball's **run and gun**) that doesn't work in the past tense. *See also* BENCH, BENCH WARMER, RIDE THE PINE.

● shirtfront

A **shirtfront** is a cricket pitch with a hard, flat, smooth surface (resembling the front of a starched shirt) that has an even, predictable bounce and is ideal for batting:

With a mediocre attack – barring Gillespie – the Australians have done a great job by claiming four wickets on a shirtfront of a wicket ideally suited for the Indian strokemakers. rediff.com, 13/12/03

● shoestring catch

In baseball, a **shoestring catch** is a spectacular running catch made very close to the feet, just before the ball would have hit the ground:

Colorado right fielder Jeromy Burnitz attempted to make a shoestring catch but the ball skipped under his glove and rolled to the warning track. usatoday.com, 11/6/04

● shoot

Beyond its use in sports such as football and hockey to describe an attempt to score, the word **shoot** has specific applications in other sports. Golfers talk about **shooting** (that is, making) a particular score for a round of golf: 'Goosen shot an 8-under 64 to move into a three-way tie for the lead.' Basketball players **shoot** baskets.

● shooter

In cricket, a **shooter** is a ball that skids very low after bouncing off the pitch, making it difficult for the batsman to play it. *See also* GRUBBER.

● shooting boots

A striker who 'has his **shooting boots** on' is in a rich vein of form, while one who 'hasn't got his shooting boots on today' or has 'left his shooting boots at home' is unable to find the back of the net. Players can 'forget' to put on their shooting boots, 'remember' to put them on, 'lose' them, 'find' them or 'discover' them:

Although [striker Craig Dargo] struggled to find the target in the early stages of the season, he eventually discovered his shooting boots and has now hit 16 goals. 4thegame.com, 24/2/06

Boots can represent not only goalscoring but also playing football generally: the player who comes to the end of his career doesn't retire, he 'hangs up his boots'.

● short game

A golfer's **short game** is how well they play on or within close range of the green: in other words, how well they pitch, chip and putt:

Lawrie spent much of the close season working on his short game. scotsman.com, 14/1/06

● short head

In British horse racing, the narrowest winning margin is a **short head**. In the US, it's a **nose**.

● shot heard round the world

In US baseball history, the **shot heard round the world** was the home run hit by the New York Giants player Bobby Thomson in the deciding game of the National League pennant play-off series against the Brooklyn Dodgers in 1951. The Giants won the game 5–4 thanks to Thomson's home run and thereby clinched the pennant. The phrase, drawn from Ralph Waldo Emerson's poem *Concord Hymn* (1837), originally referred to the Battle of Lexington and Concord, the first clash of the American Revolutionary War.

● shot in the bag

To have the ability to play every possible type of golf shot, as required, is to 'have every **shot in the bag**'. Or, if a player has to attempt a tricky shot calling for particular skill, a commentator might say 'he's got that shot in his bag'. A similar expression in football is 'in his locker', as in 'he's got everything in his locker' or 'he has that little bit of magic in his locker'. Using the clubs in the golfbag metaphorically to stand for all-round golfing proficiency is also evident in such turns of phrase as 'you need to play well right through the bag on this course'. *See also* LOCKER

● shotstopper

Sometimes the word **shotstopper** is used simply as a synonym for goalkeeper. But there is often an implied criticism in the use of the term. A goalkeeper so described may be thought to be particularly good at reacting athletically to shots but perhaps less adept at other aspects of his game, such as commanding his area and dealing with crosses and free kicks.

● shot to nothing

In snooker, a **shot to nothing** is an attempt to pot a ball where
the player knows that there is very little chance of leaving his
opponent with a good potting opportunity even if the shot is
missed.

● shoulder arms

Cricket commentators sometimes say that a batsman has
shouldered arms. When the phrase is used of a soldier it
describes the act of holding a rifle in an upright position against
the body, barrel against the shoulder. A batsman may be thought
of as a combatant and the bat he wields a weapon, but the action
here is somewhat different. The batsman deliberately raises the
bat high above his shoulders and out of the line of the ball,
judging that the ball will not hit the wicket and it is safe for him
not to attempt to play a shot.

● shout

In the context of a cricket match, a **shout** is an appeal (a call by
the fielding side asking the umpire to declare the batsman out), as
in 'the bowler had a very good shout for LBW turned down by the
umpire' or 'that was definitely worth a shout'.

● Show

In baseball slang, **the Show** is the major league, comprising the
two main North American professional baseball leagues, the
National League and the American League. In the 1988 film *Bull
Durham*, Kevin Costner's character Crash Davis says, 'Yeah, I been
in the Show. I was in the Show for twenty-one days, twenty-one
greatest days of my life.'

● showboating

Showboating, an expression often used with disapproval, is
showing off or playing to the gallery, when players draw attention

to themselves with ostentatious celebrations or flamboyant demonstrations of virtuosity, often in a way that treats their opponents with a lack of respect. Originally a US term, it derives from *showboat*, a paddle-wheel river steamer on which theatrical performances are given.

[Gallimore] brought a roar from the crowd when he lifted the football in the air and did a little showboating on his way to the 86-yard touchdown reception and a 21–0 lead. okmulgeetimes.com, 25/8/05

Sitting on a comfortable two-goal cushion, Cherries started enjoying themselves and Claus Jorgensen indulged in a spot of showboating down the right wing on a couple of occasions. scfc.co.uk, 2/4/01

See also SHAKE AND BAKE, SHOW PONY.

● show pony

Show pony is a disapproving term for a player who tries to impress with too many fancy tricks on the ball and not enough hard work or simple, effective play. Continuing the equine theme, the opposite of a show pony is perhaps a 'workhorse'.

Ronaldo may have been derided as something of a show-pony, with his tendency to over-elaborate with repeated step-overs, when he arrived at Manchester United from Portugal last summer. sportinglife.com, 22/6/04

See also FANCY DAN, SHOWBOATING.

● shunt

In motor racing, a **shunt** is a collision between cars, especially when one car runs into the back of another. British driver James Hunt was known as 'Hunt the Shunt' early in his racing career because he was involved in a large number of crashes.

● shutout

A **shutout** is the baseball equivalent of a 'clean sheet' in football. A pitcher who throws or pitches a shutout pitches a whole game without the opposing team scoring a run. The phrase **shutout ball** is also used, to describe a pitching performance during which no runs are scored: 'He pitched shutout ball through the first five innings.' The term **shutout** is also used in ice hockey, when a goaltender concedes no goals in a game. *See also* CLEAN SHEET.

shut the door

In motor racing, a driver **shuts the door** if he moves over sharply in order to prevent another car from passing:

At the following right-hander, Hill dived for the inside but Schumacher swiftly shut the door. Observer, 7/3/04

silly

Silly mid-off, silly mid-on, silly point: even people with little interest in cricket seem to be aware that some fielding positions are described, bafflingly, as **silly**. In this context, the word is a kind of modifying prefix, indicating that a fielding position is closer than usual to the batsman. Such positions are 'silly' in so far as they are perilously close to the bat.

silverware

Trophies are invariably described as **silverware**: 'we have a real chance of silverware this season', 'I expect to win silverware with this club'.

simulation

Simulation is the technical term for 'diving', that is, deliberately falling to the ground or exaggerating an injury in order to deceive the referee into awarding a foul against an opposing player.

sin bin

In sports such as rugby and ice hockey, the **sin bin** is an area off the field of play where a player who has committed a foul can be sent to sit for a specified period as a penalty during a game. The term can also be used as a verb:

In the 23rd minute England's second-rower Danny Grewcock was sin-binned for taking Alastair Kellock out off the ball. rugbyguide.com, 26/2/06

● sit

In American sport, **sit** can be used to mean specifically 'sit on the bench', that is, to be a substitute:

After Sitting, Powell Rises to the Occasion headline, Washington Post, 3/4/05

● sitter

A **sitter,** in football, is a simple goalscoring opportunity, though it is only called this when it is squandered. Sitters are always missed:

Nedved missed a sitter just before the break, skewing Del Piero's lay-off over the bar. eurosport.co.uk, 4/3/06

Sitters come in two varieties, 'complete' and 'absolute'. In cricket, a **sitter** is an easy catch, again especially when the offered chance is spurned.

● six-pointer

When two football teams in danger of relegation play each other, trying not only to secure three precious points for themselves but simultaneously deny their opponents the opportunity to gain three points of their own, such an encounter is known as a **six-pointer**. The term can also be applied to matches at the top of the table between teams vying for a championship or promotion. A six-pointer is usually described as 'real' or 'vital'. In the days when only two points were awarded for a win, the term **four-pointer** was used.

Down in the basement, bottom of the table Istres, who look doomed to relegation already, host Bastia (17) in what is a real six-pointer.
worldsoccer.about.com, 3/12/04

Bromsgrove Rovers face a vital relegation six-pointer tomorrow when they take on rock-bottom Cinderford Town at the Victoria Ground in the Dr Martens League. thisisbrfc.co.uk, 5/1/01

● skiddy

In cricket, a fast bowler or delivery is described as **skiddy** if the ball comes through to the batsman fast and low after pitching.

● skittle out

You can say a cricket side is **skittled out** if all the wickets are taken in rapid succession and for a low score:

West Indies skittled out Zimbabwe for 144 to win by 98 runs in Antigua.
bbc.co.uk, 30/4/06

● skyer

A **skyer** (or **skier**) in cricket is a ball that is hit very high into the air and comes down almost vertically, often into the hands of a fielder.

● skywalk

Basketball players who are capable not only of prodigious leaps but also lateral movement while hanging in the air are said to be able to **skywalk**. The term is particularly associated with the 1970s US basketball star David Thompson, whose astonishing leaping ability earned him his nickname 'Skywalker'.

● slam dunk

Slam dunk is a basketball term for when a player jumps up as high as the rim and thrusts the basketball down through the net with a lot of force. The term has passed into general usage in US English to mean something that is certain to happen, a foregone conclusion, as in 'this decision was a slam dunk' or 'Utah tax cut no slam dunk'. *See also* DUNK.

● sledging

Sledging is a cricketing term, probably Australian in origin, for the practice of close fielders verbally abusing or needling the batsman at the crease, with the aim of unsettling him and disrupting his concentration. The word comes from the idea of breaking down the batsman's resistance, as if battering him with a sledgehammer. The Australian cricket team also refer to sledging as 'mental disintegration'.

● sleeping giant

Sleeping giant is a label attached to a football club with substantial support and an illustrious history that has nevertheless spent several unsuccessful years out of the top division. Wolverhampton Wanderers were the archetypal sleeping giants of the 1980s and 1990s. In general usage the phrase, coined by Napoleon Bonaparte in the early 19th century to describe China, is often used to characterize large, long-dormant economic powers such as China and India. The phrase is also familiar from the supposed words of the Japanese admiral Isoroku Yamamoto after the Japanese attack on Pearl Harbor in 1941: 'I fear all we have done is awaken a sleeping giant and fill him with a terrible resolve.' Other examples of sleep-related sporting terminology include **dormie** and **wake-up call**. *See also* MASSIVE CLUB.

● slider

A **slider** in cricket is a ball bowled by a leg spin bowler that is pushed out of the front of the hand and doesn't spin as much as the batsman expects, coming on to the batsman in a straight line after pitching. In baseball, on the other hand, a **slider** is a relatively fast pitch that curves slightly in the air as it reaches the batter.

SPORTING IDIOMS

Sport provides many idiomatic expressions used in our everyday speech. For example:

baseball – *ballpark figure, bat for someone, cover all the bases, get to first base, in the right ballpark, off base, out of left field, play hardball, right off the bat, strike out, throw a curveball, touch base, whole new ballgame*

boxing – *below the belt, body blow, box clever, in your corner, on the ropes, out for the count, saved by the bell, take it on the chin, throw in the sponge (or towel)*

cricket – *break your duck, not cricket, off your own bat*

football – *have the ball at your feet, level playing field, move the goalposts, own goal*

golf – *par for the course, rub of the green*

horse racing – *also-ran, down to the wire, home stretch, win by a nose, win hands down*

pool – *behind the eight ball, call the shots*

other sports – *ball is in your court, game plan, jump the gun, keep your eye on the ball, kick into touch, play ball, take your eye off the ball, toe the line*

We use these sport-related metaphors to talk about such experiences as, for example, winning and losing (**win hands down, throw in the sponge**), strategies for achieving goals in life (**play hardball, game plan**), failure (**strike out**) and facing difficulties or obstacles (**behind the eight ball, body blow**).

● slog

A **slog** in cricket is a powerful but inelegant shot hit without great technique high into the air. A batsman who hits a lot of shots like this is a **slogger**. The final overs of a team's innings in a limited-overs match are sometimes called the **slog overs** because batsmen try to score lots of boundaries quickly rather than bothering about losing wickets.

● smash-and-grab

It is customary in football for a victory by the away side, especially one in dramatic circumstances and featuring an undeserved last-minute winner, to be termed a **smash-and-grab** or a **smash-and-grab raid**: 'United pull off Cup smash-and-grab.' Smash and Grab, incidentally, were the nicknames of the 1970s Bristol Rovers strike partnership of Alan Warboys and Bruce Bannister respectively.

● smear

In the language of cricket, to **smear** a shot is to hit it effortlessly and with power:

Warne was smeared into the stand next over by Pietersen. cricket.co.uk, 22/7/05

Shoaib returns with the gentlest of looseners, but Flintoff smears it straight to square-leg three-quarters of the way to the fence, to spoil England's lunch. bbc.co.uk, 14/11/05

● snorter

A **snorter** in cricket is an exceptionally good delivery, used particularly to refer to a fast ball that lifts sharply off the pitch:

When Stuart Clark produced a snorter to remove Herschelle Gibbs it seemed that the game might be up for the locals. smh.com.au, 29/3/06

soft goal

Fooball managers hate their team giving away **soft goals**. This is a goal conceded far too easily due to inexcusable defensive lapses.

soft hands

Soft hands in sport are usually an asset, not a sign of feebleness. In cricket, batsmen are said to play with **soft hands** when they relax their hands as they play the ball in order to strike it with a dead bat (that is, a loosely held one), particularly useful when playing spin bowling. The term is also used of fielders in both cricket and baseball who catch a ball with similarly relaxed hands so that it doesn't bounce straight out.

On a pitch lacking in bounce, he pushed his front foot out, played with soft hands in defence, but was completely assured when going for his strokes. crincinfo.com, 20/11/04

In football, a goalkeeper employs **soft hands** when he parries a goal-bound shot in such a way that the ball doesn't bounce off the hands into the path of an oncoming striker but rather is cushioned and safely deflected away from the goal.

southpaw

Southpaw, denoting a left-handed boxer who leads with his right hand, dates from the mid-19th century. In the US, a **southpaw** is a left-handed baseball pitcher, a usage that is traditionally said to derive from the east–west orientation of an old Chicago baseball park. Batters would always stand facing east to avoid looking into the late afternoon sun, so a pitcher's left hand would always be on the south side of the ballpark. More widely, the term can be applied to any left-handed person.

spider

Spiders crop up in both snooker and darts. In snooker it's the term for a long-legged rest used to assist a player in playing a shot with an awkward cueing position, while in darts it's the web-like wire grid that divides the dartboard into sections.

● spine

The **spine** of a football team is its central axis, comprising the goalkeeper, central defender, central midfielder and striker:

England should be serious contenders [for Euro 2008] with a team built around the spine of Paul Robinson, John Terry, Frank Lampard and Wayne Rooney. Observer, 22/1/06

● spit the dummy out

A horse that gives up before the end of a race can be said to **spit the dummy out**. The analogy is with an infant's temper tantrum:

The first time we worked him, he spat the dummy out and didn't want to know. Noel Wilson, trainer, racingpost.co.uk, 17/6/04

● splash and dash

In motor-racing lingo, a **splash and dash** (also known as a **splash and go**) is a quick pit stop in the closing laps of a race to take on just enough fuel to be sure of finishing the race.

● spray

A player or team that successfully passes the ball all over the pitch can be said to be **spraying** passes around, as in 'the Australians began to spray passes around' and 'he has the ability to spray pinpoint passes all over the field'.

● square ball

It doesn't sound as though it would roll very far, but the curiously termed **square ball** is a pass or cross played to another player laterally across the football pitch, neither forwards nor backwards:

Anderson Polga plays a square ball to Beto as Sporting look to work the ball out of defence. sportinglife.com, 14/4/05

Other attributes a ball can have (when it means a pass, that is) include 'good', 'quality', 'long' and 'early'.

● stayer

A **stayer** is a horse with great stamina that prefers races over longer distances. Jockeys and trainers are fond of saying that their horse 'can stay all day'.

● steal

To **steal** the ball in basketball is to gain possession of it from an opposing player. The metaphor of theft is central to many sports in which players strive to take possession of the ball away from an opponent. *See also* NICK A GOAL, POACHER, STEAL A BASE.

● steal a base

Just as football teams can **nick a goal**, baseball runners can **steal a base**, that is, sprint safely from one base to another without the ball being hit or a fielder making an error, usually starting to run just as the pitcher is delivering the pitch.

● steam in

When describing the sight of a fast bowler's run-up as he charges in to bowl, cricket writers and commentators often say that the bowler is **steaming in**.

● steepling

In cricket, the adjective 'steepling' tends to be used in conjunction with the words 'bounce' or 'catch'. A ball with **steepling bounce** rises up high off the pitch at a steep angle. A **steepling catch** is one that comes down to a fielder from a great height.

● step up to the plate

In baseball, a batter **steps up to the plate** when it is his turn to bat and he takes up his position at the home plate. The phrase has been borrowed by other sports (including, bizarrely, cricket), and indeed within the language generally, to mean 'accept a challenge or responsibility' or 'rise to the occasion'. There is perhaps the idea of a person stepping forward to volunteer for something.

The one thing that stood out for England was every time a performance was needed one of our guys stepped up to the plate. Andrew Flintoff, 13/9/05

Charles N'Zogbia has told his fellow Newcastle United fringe players they must step up to the plate in the absence of Michael Owen. icnewcastle.co.uk, 4/1/06

See also PUT YOUR HAND UP.

● sticky wicket

Sticky wicket (or **sticky dog**) is the term for a cricket pitch that is drying out in the sun after heavy rain and that, because of the degree to which the ball can be made to turn, can be an extremely difficult surface to bat on. Now that pitches are covered, sticky wickets are much less common than they used to be, particularly at first-class level, and the phrase is now more likely to be used in its figurative rather than in its literal sense. In general usage, a **sticky wicket** is a difficult or awkward situation, a meaning dating from the 1950s.

● stonewall

A **stonewall** penalty is so described by an outraged football manager who believes an incident was without question a certain penalty, particularly when it has not been given by the referee. Less frequently the adjectives 'cast-iron' or 'stone-cold' are used. The cricketing equivalent is a **plumb** LBW decision.

stop the bleedin

In golf, to **stop the bleed**
during a round. Having score
priority is to make par on the r
could do. I just couldn't stop the
named Jason Gore after scoring 84
US Open and dropping from 2nd pla

streaky

Streaky is used in cricket to describe runs tha   off the edge
of the bat, usually into an area behind the wick   as in 'he edged
a streaky four through the slips'.

strike

Football commentators often refer to a shot on goal as a **strike**,
perhaps modified by a word like 'good' or 'speculative':

*His movement was good, he was involved in most of our attacking work
and also pinched a goal with a good strike.* Mark Hughes, Blackburn
Rovers manager, 22/2/05

In cricket, whichever of the two batsmen is about to receive the
next delivery is said to be 'on strike' or to 'have the strike'.
See also FARM THE STRIKE.

strike bowler

Although the word 'strike' in cricket tends to be associated with
batsmen (who are 'on strike', 'have the strike', or 'take strike'), it
is also used in the phrase **strike bowler**, denoting an attacking
bowler whose chief role in the side is to take wickets, as opposed to
merely restricting the flow of runs from the batting side.
See also STRIKE.

atter who **strikes out** fails to hit three successive ills and is consequently called out. In general usage, to e **out** is to fail completely. *See also* WHIFF.

strike partner

In football, forwards are known as strikers, of course, and often hunt for goals in pairs. One player's fellow-striker is sometimes referred to as his **strike partner**:

Henry ensured Arsenal went in at the break with their noses in front after being played in by strike partner Jose Antonio Reyes. theage.com.au, 18/10/04

stripped

Medal-winning competitors, who subsequently have their medal taken away from them usually as a punishment for a drug violation, are always said to have been **stripped** of their medal.

stuff

Wonderfully vague, in the context of baseball **stuff** refers to the variation and speed at a pitcher's disposal. A pitcher who moves the ball around well has 'good' stuff: 'He is a big game pitcher with excellent stuff.' Interestingly, only pitchers have stuff. Batters don't.

stun

Stun is a favourite word among headline-writers, a more dramatic way of saying 'defeat', particularly (though not necessarily) when the result is an unexpected one: 'Safina Stuns Favourite Clijsters'.

stymie

Stymie used to be a golfing term, referring to a situation on the green in which the path of a player's ball to the hole was blocked by another player's ball. In 1951 the rules were changed, permitting a player to pick up an obstructing ball and mark its position. In current usage, to be **stymied** is to be hindered or thwarted. The origin of the word isn't known.

● suicide squeeze

As the name implies, a **suicide squeeze** in baseball is a highly risky manoeuvre. A runner on third base tries to run towards home plate just as the pitcher begins to deliver the ball. The runner is relying on the batter to 'lay down a bunt', that is, to play a weak shot, simply pushing the ball forwards without swinging the bat. *See also* BUNT.

● surprise package

Since the term has become something of a cliché, it is in a sense no surprise at all. But in commentator-speak, a team thought to be performing unexpectedly well in a particular season or in a tournament is inevitably dubbed the **surprise package**, as in 'Iran could be the surprise package of the World Cup finals', or 'Wigan Athletic have been this season's surprise package'.

● survival

Survival has a particular meaning in the football lexicon, referring specifically to avoiding relegation, as in 'West Brom are fighting for Premiership survival' and 'Portsmouth give their survival chances a boost'.

● sweeper

In football, a **sweeper** is a skilful defender who is tasked to play behind the other defenders, without marking duties, in order to 'sweep up' the ball should the defensive line be breached and also to help build attacking moves from the back. *See also* LIBERO.

● sweet spot

The **sweet spot** on a piece of sporting equipment such as a cricket bat, baseball bat, tennis racquet, etc. is the small area on its surface that produces maximum power for minimum effort when the ball is struck with it. There is physics involved here: it is the point of impact at which vibrations are kept to a minimum. The sweet spot is also known as the 'middle' of the bat or racquet. *See also* MAKER'S NAME, MEAT OF THE BAT, MIDDLE.

● switch hitter

A **switch hitter** is a baseball batter who can bat either right-handed or left-handed. By extension, the term can also be applied informally to a bisexual person.

t

● table setter

In baseball, a **table setter** (or a player who **sets the table**) is a batter who bats near the top of the batting order and is good at getting on base rather than being one of the more powerful hitters:

The speedster will be a prime table-setter for the Pods. nydailynews.com, 31/3/05

Damon was a sparkplug for the Red Sox, helping to set the table for power hitters David Ortiz and Manny Ramirez. eurosport.com, 23/12/05

See also CLEAR THE TABLE.

● tail wagging

Tailenders, or the **tail**, are the last four or so batsmen in a cricket side's batting line-up, usually the specialist bowlers in descending order of batting ability. Should the tail unexpectedly manage to contribute a significant number of runs between them, it is said to **wag**, one of the more delightful cricketing expressions.
See also WAGGING THE TAIL.

● take a knee

Taking a knee is a manoeuvre in American football in which a quarterback drops to one knee immediately after receiving the snap (when the ball is put into play by being passed backwards) rather than attempting to pass or run with it, as a time-wasting tactic to preserve a lead late in the game:

Donovan took a knee at the Eagles' 33-yard line and the game was over. philadelphiaeagles.com, 16/11/03

See also RUN THE CLOCK DOWN.

● take it on the chin

To **take it on the chin** is to face up to a defeat or misfortune bravely or stoically. The idiom comes from boxing, where, if a fighter receives a blow on the chin, they risk being knocked out.

● take the net

In tennis, to **take the net** is another way of saying 'attack the net', that is, to quickly advance to the front of the court towards the net so that you are in a position to hit volleys. *See also* ATTACK THE NET.

● take the positives

A staple of the post-match interview is a remark such as 'we must take the positives from this performance' or 'there are a lot of positives to come out of the game'. Now here's a curious thing: you only seem to **take the positives** out of a defeat, never a victory. The expression has almost become a euphemism for saying you've lost. The positives here are the encouraging aspects of a team's or player's performance.

● take your eye off the ball

In general usage, to **take your eye off the ball** is to fail to stay alert and keep your attention focused on what is most important.

The metaphor comes from ball games such as football, baseball, cricket and tennis. *See also* BALL-WATCHING.

● talisman

No team seems complete these days without its **talisman**, the key player whose inspirational presence and match-winning performances appear crucial to the team's success. Commentators regularly refer to 'England's talisman Andrew Flintoff' or 'Luis Figo, the talismanic figure of Portuguese football'. A talisman is literally an object thought to have magic powers and to bring good fortune, a lucky charm.

● talking horse

There was a popular American TV comedy in the 1960s called *Mister Ed*, about a horse that could talk. In horse racing, though, a **talking horse** is one that comes to a race with a lofty reputation, especially one that may not be fully justified.

● talking point

In the language of football commentary, any controversial decision or incident becomes a **talking point**, a subject for discussion after the game or at half-time: 'not only did the game have six goals but plenty of talking points too', 'the sending-off was the major talking point in a poor game.'

● tank

A slang term used in various sports, such as tennis and boxing, to **tank** is to deliberately lose a match. In tennis, tanking can sometimes involve making no further effort to win a set that appears already to be lost, with the intention of conserving energy and concentration for the next set. The allusion is to a swimming pool and the more familiar phrase 'take a dive'. **Tank** can also mean to defeat an opponent heavily, as in 'last season we gave them a 5–1 tanking'. *See also* GO IN THE TANK.

● tape-measure shot

A **tape-measure shot** in baseball is one hit such a long distance that it might be necessary to get a tape-measure out and measure it in case any records have been broken.

● target man

In football, a **target man** is a tall, strong striker who is the 'target' for long, high passes upfield from his team's own half. The typical target man tends to be good at heading the ball and has the ability to 'hold the ball up' so that teammates have time to join in the attacking move. *See also* OUT-AND-OUT STRIKER

● tester

In golf, a **tester** is a tricky little putt, likely to be holed but nevertheless not quite a **gimme**: 'He missed the putt and left himself with a tester for par.'

● Texas wedge

Texas wedge is golf slang for a putter when used from off the green, for example in windy conditions. Such approach shots are common in some parts of Texas because of the windy climate and the hard, dry ground.

● thread the needle

To **thread the needle** in American football is to pass the ball to a teammate through a small gap between two defending players from the opposing team:

Favre's bullet threaded the needle between the two Cincinnati defenders and landed right on Taylor's hands with 13 seconds showing.
jsonline.com, 18/9/02

SUBSTITUTES

There is a rich lexicon of terms associated with the **substitutes' bench** (or **subs' bench**), where the reserve players who have not been chosen as part of the starting line-up sit. Not only is such a player said to be **on the bench**, but the word **bench** itself can be used as a synonym for a team's substitutes as a group: 'they have a strong bench', 'there's lots of pace on the bench'. A player denied a starting place in the team is **benched**. If he subsequently 'comes on as a substitute' to replace another player, he is said to **come off the bench**. A particularly effective substitute, who frequently **scores off the bench**, is sometimes described as a **super-sub**.

Many expressions focus on the physical experience of sitting down while a game or match is in progress. Indeed, being a substitute can be described simply as **sitting** in US usage, and substitutes in such sports as baseball, American football and basketball can also be said to **warm the bench**, **ride the bench**, **ride the pine** or **shine the pine**. These are the **bench players** or (when they get few opportunities to play) **bench warmers**. The best of the substitutes on a basketball team, first choice to come onto the court, is the **sixth man**.

● Thrilla in Manila

The **Thrilla in Manila** was the promotional nickname given to a world heavyweight title fight between Muhammad Ali and Joe Frazier held in Quezon City in the Philippines, just outside Manila, on 1 October 1975. The rhyming nickname was consciously based on the 'Rumble in the Jungle' the previous year. Ali won the Thrilla in Manila, an epic, bruising contest, to retain the title. *See also* RUMBLE IN THE JUNGLE, WAR ON THE SHORE.

● throat ball

It sounds dangerous, and it is. In cricket, a **throat ball** is a bouncer (a fast short-pitched ball) that rears up off the pitch towards the batsman's throat. *See also* CHIN MUSIC.

● throw a curveball

In baseball, a **curveball** is a slower pitch thrown with spin so that it deviates from a straight path and drops sharply as it reaches the batter. In general usage, if someone **throws you a curveball**, they catch you off guard with a difficult or unexpected question or task.

● throwing

In cricket parlance, **throwing** is bowling with an illegal action in which the elbow is straightened more than a permitted number of degrees during a delivery. According to the laws of cricket, a ball is fairly bowled if 'once the bowler's arm has reached the level of the shoulder in the delivery swing, the elbow joint is not straightened partially or completely from that point until the ball has left the hand'. *See also* CHUCKER.

● throw in the towel/sponge

To **throw in the towel** or **the sponge** (or, indeed, **throw up the sponge**) means 'to give in or admit defeat'. These expressions come from the boxing ring: a boxer's trainer or second throws a towel or sponge into the middle of the ring as a sign that he admits his boxer has been beaten and so it is time for the boxing match to be stopped by the referee.

● tickle

A batsman who gets a **tickle** (or **tickles** the ball) hits the ball with the bat with the faintest of edges:

Vaas tickles a leg-side Hoggard delivery to complete his fifty. bbc.co.uk, 15/5/06

● tifosi

Italian sports fans, particularly the fanatical supporters of the Italian motor-racing team Ferrari, are known as **tifosi**. The word derives from the Italian word for the fever typhus.

● timbers

Used mainly by cricket journalists, **timbers** is a rather old-fashioned term for the stumps:

Armed with the old ball, Kasprowicz ended Marvan Atapattu's contribution with a late swinger that invited the off drive and broke between bat and pad to rattle the timbers. theage.com.au, 27/3/04

See also CRASH OF ASH.

● Timeless Test

The phrase **Timeless Test** refers to the 1939 cricket Test match between England and South Africa played in Durban. After nine days of play (plus two rest days) in which an aggregate of 1,981 runs were scored, the match was eventually abandoned as a draw because the England team had to leave Durban to get their steamship back home, the captain of which couldn't wait any longer.

● tinker

A football manager who tends to make frequent changes to his
team's line-up, formation and tactics risks being accused of
tinkering. The doyen of tinkerers was Claudio Ranieri, who earned
the nickname 'the Tinkerman' while Chelsea manager 2000–4 for
constantly shuffling his squad of players.

● to be fair

A popular verbal tic with ex-players contributing to radio and TV
football commentaries as pundits, **to be fair** doesn't always mean
what you might expect it to mean. Instead of being used, like 'in
all fairness', when adding a comment to excuse a player for an
error on the pitch or to mitigate criticism, the phrase has become
for some a substitute for 'to be honest' or 'as it happens'. So far
from being conciliatory, it may be signalling that the speaker is in
fact being quite critical or outspoken, as in 'he's had a shocker of
a game, to be fair'. This can be confusing for the listener. Former
Newcastle and Liverpool striker Peter Beardsley is a notorious
'to-be-fairer'.

● toe

In horse-racing slang, a horse's **toe** (also called its **turn of foot**)
is its speed or acceleration.

● toe the line

The expression **toe the line**, meaning 'conform to the usual rules
or attitudes, especially unwillingly', may come from the idea of
competitors in a foot race having to line up at the start with the
tips of their toes touching the starting line.

● tomato can

In boxing slang, a **tomato can** is a professional boxer of only
limited ability, often outclassed in fights. The term presumably

originates from the idea of blood spurting from such a boxer's head like a burst tomato can. *See also* HAM AND EGGER, PALOOKA.

● ton

In informal British English, a **ton** is a century, a score of 100 runs by a batsman in an innings.

● tonk

Used especially in cricket and football, the pleasingly onomato-poeic verb **tonk** means to hit or kick the ball hard: 'Brett Lee was tonked for 27 runs in his last two overs.' **Tonk** can also mean to inflict a heavy defeat on another team, to trounce them: 'They tonked us 4–1 last season.'

● tools of ignorance

The **tools of ignorance** are a grandly ironic term for a baseball catcher's protective gear, including a helmet with a faceguard, a chest protector, shin guards and a padded glove (called a mitt).

● top flight

Football journalists are fond of the term **top flight** to denote the highest level in the league: 'this is Wigan's first season in the top flight', 'he is relishing a return to top-flight football'. The term usefully covers not only the Premier League (founded in 1992) but also its predecessor, the old First Division.

● top of the ground

A racehorse that prefers to run on firm ground can be said to be best **on top of the ground** or described as a **top-of-the-ground** horse. *See also* MUDLARK.

● tops

Double 20, the segment of a dartboard right at the top, is colloquially known as **tops**, as in 'you need tops to win'. *See also* DOUBLE TOP.

● total football

The phrase **total football** (*totaal voetbal* in Dutch) is used to describe a fluid, attractive, attacking style of play pioneered by Rinus Michels, manager of Ajax and the Dutch national team in the early 1970s. In this system, none of the outfield players had a fixed position and all were adaptable enough to interchange positions freely around the pitch, with the result that any player could be involved in free-flowing attacking moves.

● touch

A player admired for having 'great **touch**' or 'perfect touch' is able to exercise precise and delicate control when striking a ball or making a shot. The term is used widely in sports such as golf, tennis, basketball and football.

● touch base

To **touch base** is to briefly make contact or keep in touch with someone, an expression that derives from baseball. A baseball player who is physically touching one of the bases is not in danger of being put out. *See also* COVER ALL THE BASES, GET TO FIRST BASE, OFF BASE.

● track

Cricketers sometimes refer to the pitch as the **track**, as in 'a good batting track', 'a spinning track' or 'a flat track'.

● traffic

A number of sporting expressions fall into the bluff sport-as-a-job category, including **bad day at the office** and **go looking for**

work. Racing drivers make themselves sound like delayed commuters when they describe slow-moving cars at the back of the field as **traffic**:

I got held up in traffic before the second pit stop, which cost me a lot.
Fernando Alonso, 10/7/05

In sports such as rugby and American football, the word **traffic** (often in the phrase 'heavy traffic') denotes a crowded area of the pitch where a large number of opposing players are suddenly on hand to impede progress:

Barry Murphy went past two tackles but ran into heavy traffic inside the Ulster half. limerick-leader.ie, 11/3/06

Tom Voyce made a superb 50 metre break from deep inside his own half, but took the wrong option to head infield into traffic when an offload to his right would have sent Josh Lewsey over unopposed.
skysports.com, 31/12/05

● tramlines

The **tramlines** are a pair of parallel lines that mark the sides of a tennis court, the inside line defining the boundary of a singles court, the outside one a doubles court.

● trapdoor

The **trapdoor** is a potent metaphor as the end of the football season approaches and teams near the bottom of the table face the prospect of relegation to the division below. These teams are anxious to avoid 'falling' or 'dropping' through the **relegation trapdoor**. A related expression is 'facing the drop'. *See also* DROP, DROP ZONE.

● travel well

In horse racing, a horse that **travels well** is a good performer needing little urging from the jockey.

● trey

A **trey** is a shot in basketball that scores three points, an extension of the word's much older meaning, for a playing card or dice throw with three spots.

● trip

Trip is a horse-racing term referring both to the distance of a race and to a horse's ability to complete the course. A horse is said to **get the trip** if it is able to stay the distance of the race.

● truck and trailer

Truck and trailer is a piece of rugby jargon used to describe a form of obstruction in which the player with the ball holds on to the back of a teammate as they move forwards, the player in front (that is, the 'truck') shielding the ball-carrier (that is, the 'trailer') from tacklers.

● trundler

The rather disparaging term **trundler** describes a slow-medium pace bowler who is reliable but unexciting. There is a suggestion that the bowler moves heavily or laboriously as he runs in to bowl.

● turn your arm over

To **turn your arm over** in cricket is to bowl, but the expression is generally used in the context of a player who is only an infrequent bowler:

With things not happening for the regular spinners, India brought in Sachin Tendulkar to turn his arm over in the 58th over. ia.rediff.com, 11/12/05

I did a bit more than turn my arm over this winter and I think it's something I'm definitely going to have to do more of, for the good make-up of the team. Kevin Pietersen, 3/5/06

tweener

In basketball, the tallest players tend to play in the area around the basket. These are the forwards. Shorter, faster players mainly play away from the basket, being skilled at dribbling and passing. These are the guards. And then there are the **tweeners**, who come 'in between', not quite tall enough or fast enough to specialize in either position, but versatile enough to be able to play in more than one position on the court. The form of the word closely resembles the archaic word *tweeny*, a maid who assisted both the cook and the housemaid, and was thus a 'between-maid'.

twin killing

In baseball, a double play, a series of actions in which two opposing players are put out, is informally known as a **twin killing**.

twirler

Twirler is a cricket journalists' word for a spin bowler, as in 'South African twirler Paul Adams'.

u

Uncle Charlie

One of the more curious terms used in baseball for a curveball (a pitched ball with a curving trajectory) is **Uncle Charlie**, apparently deriving from CB radio usage in the 1970s.
See also DEUCE, YAKKER.

unforced error

A phrase that could be used during many sporting contests but is mostly associated with tennis, an **unforced error** is a situation during play in which a player loses a point by playing a poor shot into the net or out of the court, rather than as a result of pressure from a good shot played by the other player.

up and down

To get **up and down** in golf is to get the ball in the hole from somewhere off the green in two strokes, that is, a pitch or chip (up onto the green) followed by a single putt (down into the hole): 'From there it's almost impossible to get it up and down for your par.' The term can also be used as a noun, as in 'a brilliant up-and-down from the greenside rough'.

up-and-under

In rugby, an **up-and-under** is a very high kick that keeps the ball in the air long enough for the kicker and his teammates to rush forwards to catch it and which is intended to put pressure on the defending player trying to catch the ball. The expression was popularized in the 1960s and 1970s by the rugby commentator Eddie Waring. *See also* GARRYOWEN.

up the jumper

Up-the-jumper rugby is a disparaging term for an unadventurous style of play that relies almost exclusively on the pack of forwards keeping possession of the ball and driving it forwards, as opposed to the more entertaining and free-flowing passing-and-running game: 'The pack will stick the ball up the jumper and try to grind out a victory.'

useful

Useful is a useful word in cricket, an all-purpose adjective to register approval for a significant contribution with bat or ball, particularly one that could be considered a bonus. So a specialist batsman may also be a 'useful bowler' or a specialist bowler a 'useful lower-order batsman':

The clincher for Blackwell, of course, is that he should be able to contribute useful runs at No 8. Guardian, 20/2/06

V

vision

Vision in sport is not simply a matter of eyesight. It is the ability of a player to see opportunities for a teammate to be brought into play, say with a perfectly judged pass. Such awareness is often preceded by an adjective like 'good', 'great' or 'real', though the word can also be used on its own.

Rooney's touch and vision brought the ball to the receptive feet of Giggs.
Daily Telegraph, 2/2/05

Stephen Ireland showed real vision as he spotted the striker lurking on the edge of the area. Sunday Mirror, 8/1/06

volley

In tennis or football, a **volley** is the playing of a shot or kicking of a ball before the ball hits the ground.

W

wagging the tail

According to a vivid and amusing item of horse-racing slang, the horse bringing up the rear in a race can be said to be **wagging the tail**. It's a curious reversal of the cricketing expression 'the tail wagging'. *See also* LANTERNE ROUGE, TAIL WAGGING.

wake-up call

A **wake-up call** is a warning that a team or player is too complacent or performing below par and needs urgently to address the situation. Events that may 'serve as' or 'act as' a wake-up call include a goal conceded early in a game or a defeat or poor performance only a short time before an important match: 'the goal served as a wake-up call for Rangers, who had started the game sluggishly', 'the 4–1 defeat against Denmark was a wake-up call for England ahead of the World Cup qualifier against Wales'.

walk

In cricket, a game mainly concerned with runs, it is considered sporting practice to **walk**. This is done by a batsman who walks away from the stumps and heads for the pavilion, having accepted that he is out without waiting for the umpire's decision.

● War on the Shore

The Ryder Cup (a golf tournament contested between teams from the US and Europe) was held in 1991 on Kiawah Island, South Carolina. In the build-up to the tournament, this was billed as the **War on the Shore** by gung-ho US golf journalists, referring to the ongoing Gulf War and echoing similarly rhyming nicknames such as the 'Rumble in the Jungle' and the 'Thrilla in Manila'. *See also* RUMBLE IN THE JUNGLE, THRILLA IN MANILA.

● wear the collar

A batter who is unfortunate enough to **wear the collar** fails to hit the ball in a game of baseball. Not only does a collar resemble the figure zero, it calls to mind the idea of choking. *See also* CHOKE, GOLDEN SOMBRERO.

● wheelhouse

In baseball, if a batter receives a pitch 'in his **wheelhouse**' it is just where the batter likes it, around waist-high and right over the middle of the plate, where the batter swings with most power. A number of baseball terms are of nautical origin and this may be another example. A vessel's wheelhouse is the structure on the bridge where the wheel is housed. Alternatively, the term may derive from another meaning of *wheelhouse*, a circular building (also called a roundhouse) used for repairing railway locomotives, containing a huge powerful turntable. *See also* AROUND THE HORN, ON DECK.

● wheelsucker

Wheelsucker is a disparaging term for a competitor in a cycling road race who sticks like a limpet to the rear wheel of the rider immediately in front, saving energy by reducing the effects of wind resistance, and refusing to do his share of the work at the front.

TABLOID HEADLINES

Sport headlines, particularly in tabloid newspapers, make use of a terse vocabulary of hyperbole intended to bring drama and impact to the story. A meeting between two teams, for example, tends to be described as a **clash**. One team doesn't merely defeat another; they **stun** them or **sink** them. A big team beaten by a smaller team is a **scalp**. Such a result is a **shock**. A competitor doesn't merely get knocked out of a tournament; they **crash out** or get **dumped** out of it. Victory is accompanied by **joy**, defeat by **woe** or **agony**. An attempt to win a title or break a record is a **bid**.

● When seagulls follow the trawler...

In January 1995, the French footballer Eric Cantona was sent off in a match between his team Manchester United and Crystal Palace. On his way off the pitch, Cantona launched a martial-arts-style kick on an allegedly abusive fan in the crowd, for which he received a conviction for assault and a sentence of community service. In the aftermath, Cantona attended a press conference at which he delivered the enigmatic observation, '**When the seagulls follow the trawler,** it is because they think sardines will be thrown into the sea'. Presumably a comment intended to compare the press pack to a flock of scavengers, it has become a much-repeated quotation.

● whiff

In baseball, to **whiff** is to **strike out**, that is, to swing and miss three times. The word has a similar meaning in golf, where it means to miss the ball completely, to play an air-shot.

● whole new ballgame

In everyday usage, a **whole new ballgame** is a completely new situation, utterly different from the previous one. The expression comes from baseball (the ballgame in question), where it denotes a dramatic turn of events in a game.

● wicket

Confusingly, the word **wicket** has a number of quite distinct meanings in the game of cricket. It can denote the stumps at either end of the pitch ('hit the wicket'). An extension of this meaning is the act of getting a batsman out ('take a wicket', 'two wickets fell in quick succession'). But the word can also refer both to a batsman's stint at the crease ('he doesn't give up his wicket easily') and to the period when two batsman are batting together ('they added 120 for the eighth wicket'). So the word can mean both getting out and not getting out. And, if that wasn't enough, it can also be used to refer to the pitch stretching out between the two sets of stumps.

● win by a nose

In horse racing, a 'nose' is the shortest possible winning distance. Figuratively, to **win by a nose** is to win a contest by a very narrow margin. *See also* NOSE.

● win hands down

Why does **win hands down** mean 'win easily'? The expression derives from horse racing: a jockey is able to lower his hands when he is winning a race comfortably.

● winner

A **winner** is an unreturnable shot that brings a tennis rally to an end and wins the point, as in 'hit a forehand volley for a winner'.

● winningest

In American sport **winningest** means most successful or winning most often, as in 'the winningest coach in NBA history' or 'the winningest team in baseball'. *See also* LOSINGEST.

● win ugly

'Patriots Win Ugly', read a US headline in 2005. Pragmatic managers and coaches will admit that they are prepared for their teams to **win ugly** on occasion, that is, to grind out a victory without playing well and certainly without any style or flair. Note that the adjective 'ugly' is pressed into service as an adverb here. The opposite is to **win pretty**. In January 2006 BBC radio commentator Alan Green accused Bolton Wanderers of playing 'ugly football' that he wouldn't pay to watch, infuriating manager Sam Allardyce.

I said to the players last week I would like them to win ugly and they certainly won very ugly today. That was the ugliest I've seen since the ugly sisters fell out of the ugly tree. Terry Butcher, Motherwell manager, 10/12/05

● woodwork

Shots that hit a goalpost or crossbar are invariably said to hit (or rattle) the **woodwork**. It can often sound as though the goal frame is playing quite an active part in the match: 'the woodwork came to their rescue again', 'we twice had the woodwork to thank in the last five minutes'.

● wrong'un

In British English a **wrong'un** is a person of bad character or a cheat. Extending the idea of dishonest fakery to a spinning cricket ball, Australians use the term as a synonym of 'googly', the leg spin bowler's deceptive delivery that turns the opposite way to the way the batsman is expecting it to turn. *See also* GOOGLY.

x y z

X-rated

Particularly violent tackles, not for the faint-hearted, may be classified as **X-rated**: 'there were plenty of X-rated tackles flying in', 'the first half was X-rated stuff'. Before 1983 films considered suitable for adults only were given an X classification.

yahoo

In cricket, a **yahoo** is a wild swing with the bat intended to launch the ball into the stands but failing to make contact. The term presumably derives from the joyous or exuberant yell 'yahoo!' rather than from the older meaning of a noisy or uncouth person (coined by Jonathan Swift in *Gulliver's Travels*). Yahoo is, of course, also the name of an internet search engine, as is Google, another piece of cricketing jargon. *See also* GOOGLE.

yakker

Yakker is baseball slang for a curveball (a pitched ball with a curving trajectory). The word derives from *yawker*, a name for a yellow-shafted woodpecker.

yard

Speed in sport is generally measured by the **yard**. So a footballer 'has an extra yard of pace' or, if not fully fit, 'looks a yard off the pace'. A fast bowler appears 'a yard quicker' than he was last season or searches for 'an extra yard of pace'. As a yard is, of course, a measure of distance not speed, it is presumably short for yard-per-second.

● yips

The dreaded **yips** is a condition that can afflict golfers, causing them to miss short putts. Characterized by twitching or involuntary jerking of the hands when about to make a putt, it is thought to be caused by nervous tension. The German golfer Bernard Langer and the Scot Sam Torrance both struggled to overcome bouts of the yips at various times during their careers. It isn't certain where this curious word originated, but its use dates back to the 1960s.

● yorker

A **yorker** in cricket is a fast delivery that is aimed to pitch close to the batsman's toes and pass underneath his bat. It is a notoriously difficult ball for the batsman to keep from hitting the base of his stumps. The origin of the term, dating back to the 1860s, is likely to be an old expression 'to put yorkshire on' someone, meaning to cheat or deceive them. To **york** a batsman is to bowl a yorker at them. *See also* BLOCKHOLE.

● You cannot be serious

One of US tennis player John McEnroe's most famous on-court outbursts occurred during his first-round match against Tom Gullikson at Wimbledon in 1981. Disputing a call of out on one of his serves, and convinced that he had seen dust fly up as the ball bounced on the line, McEnroe launched a now infamous tirade at the umpire: 'You can't be serious man. **You cannot be serious!** The ball was on the line! Chalk flew up!' *See also* CHALK.

● Your boys took one hell of a beating

When Norway beat England 2–1 in Oslo in a World Cup qualifier in September 1981, the Norwegian TV commentator Bjorge

Lillelien could not contain his jubilation: 'Lord Nelson! Lord
Beaverbrook! Sir Winston Churchill! Sir Anthony Eden! Clement
Attlee! Henry Cooper! Lady Diana! Maggie Thatcher – can you
hear me Maggie Thatcher? **Your boys took one hell of a
beating!** Your boys took one hell of a beating!' This eclectic roll-
call of quintessentially English names has become the template for
the gloating celebration and has been much parodied, with other
countries' national icons taking the place of Winston Churchill *et
al.* For example, when South Korea knocked Spain out of the 2002
World Cup, the *Sunday Mail*'s headline was: 'Julio Iglesias, General
Franco, Manuel from Fawlty Towers, Salvador Dali, El Cordobes,
Don Quixote de la Mancha... your boys took a hell of a beating.'
An even closer echo appeared on the Londonist website in July
2005 following the news that London had been chosen as the city
to host the 2012 Olympic Games, pipping the favourite Paris:
'Napoleon, Francois Mitterand, Charles de Gaulle, Eric Cantona,
Serge Gainsbourg, Gustave Eiffel, Johnny Halliday!!! Jacques
Chirac. Can you hear me Jacques Chirac? Your boys took one hell
of a beating. Your boys took one hell of a beating.'

● yo-yo club

A **yo-yo club** is one that regularly moves up and down between
two divisions or leagues, following alternate promotions and
relegations. Examples of football clubs that have oscillated
between the First Division and the Premier League in this way,
too good for one, not good enough for the other, include in recent
years Sunderland, Leicester City and Manchester City.

● zooter

The splendid word **zooter** denotes, in cricket, a type of delivery
bowled by a leg spinner, a ball that is pushed out of the hand with
very little spin and tends to dip late in its flight. Both the word
and the delivery originated with the Australian spinner Shane
Warne.